THE IMAGE
OF THE CITY
IN MODERN
LITERATURE

PRINCETON ESSAYS
IN LITERATURE

For a list of titles in the series,
see pages 167-168

THE IMAGE
OF THE CITY
IN MODERN
LITERATURE

by Burton Pike

PRINCETON UNIVERSITY PRESS

Copyright © 1981 by Princeton University Press
Published by Princeton University Press, Princeton, New Jersey
In the United Kingdom: Princeton University Press, Guildford, Surrey

All Rights Reserved
Library of Congress Cataloging in Publication Data will be
found on the last printed page of this book

Publication of this book has been aided by a grant from
The Paul Mellon Fund of Princeton University Press
This book has been composed in Linotron Palatino

Clothbound editions of Princeton University Press books
are printed on acid-free paper, and binding materials are
chosen for strength and durability

Printed in the United States of America by Princeton
University Press, Princeton, New Jersey

FOR
Marion AND *Leslie*
MY PARENTS

CONTENTS

PREFACE

The city in Western culture has always been problematic. It is an artifact deeply rooted in our civilization and the Western mind; there is no way of experiencing, observing, or writing about it which does not arouse strong feelings and vivid associations. The city always speaks, and with many voices. It has been a powerful image in literature since literature began: Whenever writers have chosen to use it, they have evoked and orchestrated responses with many overtones for both themselves and their readers.

As an image, the city is too large and complex to be thought of as only a literary trope. It has a double reference, to the artifact in the outside world and to the spectrum of refractions it calls into being in the minds of author and reader. The associations of "city" are already highly charged for a reader before he picks up a book which has a city in it. Within the literary work this image becomes part of a coherent system of signs, and its meanings may be only tenuously involved with the empirical city itself. The real city may furnish the material for the literary myth, but it is not a myth by itself; mythic value is imputed to it. Art originates in the mind of the artist rather than in the outside world; he arranges elements from that world to correspond to an idea which he has first conceived, and which expresses through conventions latent or unarticulated attitudes of his audience. The use of the city as a literary image is an illustration of Alfred Lange's argument that "all aesthetic pleasure in art is rooted in our oscillation between two series of associations, those of reality and those of art."[1] The many links between the real city and the word-city are indirect and complex, and not, as they might at first appear, simple references from one to the other. A large part of the interest of this subject lies in the connection between the reader's unarticulated attitudes and the literary code which activates them.

I have tried to respect the complexity of these links between reality and image by relating literature to other disciplines, principally sociology and psychology, in an open structure. The chapters of this book were conceived as a series of thematically related essays rather than a closed unit; my intention is to show how literature can contribute to the understanding of culture rather than to write a work of literary criticism. This explains my choice of method, a technique of juxtaposition of individual examples of the image of the city from a variety of sources. Removing these instances from their immediate setting and placing them in different functional contexts allows patterns to emerge more clearly and also allows the reader to relate the argument to works and periods not dealt with here.

Real cities have had their own individual histories. They have been plagued and bombed, moved and refounded, expanded and contracted, and been subjected to all the vicissitudes of real objects in the world. On the other hand, the associations and resonances of the city as an image, especially in literature, seem to reflect attitudes which appear to have changed little since the beginning of Western culture. Some historical cities have become myths in literature at certain times but not at others, whereas other cities have rarely or never caught the artist's imagination. Cities which have become mythicized have usually been political or cultural capitals, or important cities with striking physical features. But the mythic associations seem to be consistent within a broad range through all the historical differences and changes in cultural emphasis, from the time of the early epics and the Old and New Testaments.

I am not convinced that these constant associations and attitudes correspond to a universal archetype; rather, I hold with Max Weber that our concept of the city is a unique product of Western civilization, and hence reflects a psychology— including a more limited conception of archetype—which is culturally determined. How such mental attitudes are transmitted from generation to generation or age to age is a difficult problem for modern psychology. Since this book is concerned with the associations of a figural image, its task is easier. Within the context of art, the most reasonable explanation for this apparent continuity of associations seems to lie in Gombrich's concept of the schema or adapted stereotype, according to which the artist does not mimetically paint what he sees, but makes what he sees correspond to a relational model in his mind.[2] This model relies on pre-existing schemata which are, in effect, the cultural conventions of a historical period, and which are usually slow to change.

Since my approach to the city is based on Western cultural conventions and psychological patterns, I have limited this study to the city in Western civilization. The city in the Far East is tied, at least historically, to a different set of conventions—a quite different set, Max Weber has argued, lacking the conceptions of an urban citizenry and an urban community essential to Western thinking about the city.[3] Although these differences may have lessened in recent times, to investigate them would call for a different kind of study from the present one.

The thread running through this book is the idea of the city as a paved solitude. This fine phrase of Hawthorne's, like the urban art of de Chirico, Magritte, and Escher, expresses a paradox verging on oxymoron. The city is a highly developed

xi

form of social organization on a large scale; it is inescapably a community, however defined. Yet during the nineteenth century the literary city came more and more to express the isolation or exclusion of the individual from a community, and in the twentieth century to express the fragmentation of the very concept of community. This powerful paradox is very strange, and not so easy to explain as one might at first suppose. The city as a paved solitude is the modern expression of what seems to have been throughout Western history the most powerful constant associated with the idea of "city": ambivalence, the inability of strong negative and positive impulses toward a totemic object to resolve themselves.[4]

Schematically, the history of the city in Western culture can be divided into five periods, in each of which the structure and organization of the city is differentiated from the others: the ancient city, the medieval city, the Renaissance city, the industrial city, and what we weakly call, for want of a better name, the post-industrial city. The ancient Western city ranged from seat of empire to *polis*; church and guilds largely determined the structure and quality of life in the medieval city, whereas the heady expansion of culture and commerce distinguished the European city of the Renaissance. The nineteenth century saw the rise of the industrial city, whose leading characteristic—capitalistic speculation for profit—derived from the explosion of that volatile chemical compound Balzac called "money oxide." The post-industrial city of the present is diffuse and decentralized, a "nowhere city," as Alison Lurie has tagged Los Angeles. Contemporary urban sociologists like to speak of "megalopolises," "commutersheds," and "conurbations," and clearly prefer the adjective "urban" to the noun "city."

Both the archetypal and historical implications of the word-city seem to emerge most clearly in nineteenth- and twentieth-century European and American literature, the central focus of this book. The rapid and dislocating changes brought about in that period by the unparalleled growth of capital, industrialization, population, and social theory led to a widespread self-conscious awareness of historical and social relativity. In the minds of many people there was for the first time an overt linking of the city with cultural and personal anxiety, a growing despair over the increasing difficulty of achieving a balanced relationship between the individual person and his social environment. Attitudes toward the city in nineteenth-century literature tend to affirm the negative feelings and associations which had always been present in this powerful topos, and to neglect—perhaps unfairly, as Robert Nisbet argues—the positive aspects of city life.

The first chapter sketches the early appearance of the city in literature, and demonstrates how ambivalence has been associated with the city since the beginning of Western civilization. The second and third chapters concentrate on problems associated with the word-city in European and American literature from the eighteenth to the early twentieth century. These chapters demonstrate how the general presentation of the city during this time changed from that of an essentially static object, fixed in space, to that of a fragmented and subjective kaleidoscope, constantly shifting in time. The fourth chapter deals with the paradoxical contrast between the city as locus of the alienated individual and the undifferentiated masses in late nineteenth- and early twentieth-century literature. The final chapter argues that the city as a spatial phenomenon is in profound conflict with time as the dominating convention of thought in our present society, and that this conflict, evident in sociology as well as literature, amounts to another expression of ambivalence. This chapter also discusses the background of spatial disorientation which is such a prominent thematic feature of twentieth-century writing about the city.

One path of investigation already sufficiently studied, in my opinion, and hence only peripherally mentioned in this book, is the theme of city versus country. This topos is essentially part of the pastoral tradition. Seeing the city in that context has deflected attention from the enormous power the image of the city has exercised on the human imagination by itself, independently from that tradition. It is also worth noting that most of the literature praising country over city life has been written by urbanites for urban audiences.

The sociological literature on the city is vast, the literary criticism considerable, and the quality of much of both is impressive. My notes document my indebtedness, but I would like to single out four studies which have strongly influenced the shape and thrust of this one: Donald Fanger's *Dostoevsky and Romantic Realism*, E. H. Gombrich's *Art and Illusion*, Robert Nisbet's *Sociology as an Art Form*, and Lewis Mumford's *The City in History*. All these books are boundary studies attempting to place particular problems in a larger framework and point the way to dialogues among separate disciplines of study.

If I had not lived in, and worked for, New York City during the most traumatic period in its history, I doubt if this work would have taken its present form. The city's crisis brought to the surface and frequently dramatized the normally subliminal attitudes of America's citizens—the word derives from "city"—toward the city which is both the center and the symbol of this nation's cultural life. It is not often that a writer has the opportunity to see his academic subject come to life in this fashion. Apart from that, this book was written in extremely trying academic circumstances. I am, however, most grateful to individual friends and colleagues at Queens College for their generous advice and encouragement, especially Frederick Buell, Ruth Ann Crowley, Vincent Crapanzano, Lillian Feder, and A. Robert Towers, Jr., and also to my students at Queens and at the Graduate School of the City University of New York, whose enthusiasm has been a much appreciated source of support.

xiv

I am also very grateful to Dorothy Reisman for typing the manuscript.

The lithograph by M. C. Escher, "Concave and Convex," on the dust jacket, is reproduced by permission of the Escher Foundation, Haags Gemeentemuseum, The Hague; reproduction rights arranged courtesy of the Vorpal Galleries, New York, San Francisco, Laguna Beach. The text of Georg Heym's "Der Gott der Stadt" has been taken with permission from Georg Heym, *Dichtungen und Schriften: Gesamtausgabe*. Band I: *Lyrik*. Hrsg. von Karl Ludwig Schneider. (c) 1964 Ellermann Verlag, München 19. The text of Bertolt Brecht's "Vom armen B. B." has been taken with permission from *Bertolt Brecht: Poems, 1913-1956*, ed. John Willet and Ralph Manheim, with the cooperation of Erich Fried, 1979 (c. 1976), Methuen Inc., New York.

BURTON PIKE
New York
July, 1980

THE IMAGE
OF THE CITY
IN MODERN
LITERATURE

CHAPTER I

The City as Image

The crowd had rolled back and were now huddled
together nearly at the extremity of the street, while
the soldiers had advanced no more than a third of its
length. The intervening space was empty—a paved
solitude between lofty edifices, which threw almost
a twilight shadow over it.

—HAWTHORNE, "THE GRAY CHAMPION"

Since there has been literature, there have been cities in literature. We unthinkingly consider this phenomenon modern, but it goes back to early epic and mythic thought. We cannot imagine *Gilgamesh*, the Bible, the *Iliad*, or the *Aeneid*, without their cities, which contain so much of their energy and radiate so much of their meaning. Small settlements and villages had, then as now, some direct connection to the land around them, and provided clear and limited social functions. But cities were from the beginning something special. As centers of religious and military power, as well as of social life on a large scale, they were things apart.

The city has always been man's single most impressive and visible achievement. It is a human artifact which has become an object in the world of nature. Cities are a plural phenomenon: There are many of them, but though each has its individual history, they all seem to exemplify similar patterns.

The most basic of these is the interpenetration of past and present. On the one hand there is the visible city of streets and buildings, frozen forms of energy fixed at different times in the past and around which the busy kinetic energy of the present swirls. On the other hand there are the subconscious currents arising in the minds of the city's living inhabitants from this combination of past and present. These currents include the city's ties with the realm of the dead through its temples, cemeteries, and ceremonies as well as its old buildings, and also its functions as the seat of secular power, embodied in kings, governments, and banks. Northrop Frye, following Kierkegaard's concept of repetition as re-creation, writes that "the culture of the past is not only the memory of mankind, but our own buried life, and study of it leads to a recognition scene, a discovery in which we see, not our past lives, but the cultural form of our present life."[1] The city is, as Joseph Rykwert characterizes it, a curious artifact "compounded of willed and random elements, imperfectly controlled."[2] It has even been called "a state of mind."[3]

The city has been used as a rhetorical topos throughout the history of Western culture. But it has another aspect as well, whose referent seems to be a deep-seated anxiety about man's relation to his created world. The city crystallizes those conscious and unconscious tensions which have from the beginning characterized the city in Western culture. Only such a crystallization can explain man's deep preoccupation with the city, or account for the hypnotic attraction of its destruction since Troy, Sodom and Gomorrah, and Carthage.

"Man constructs according to an archetype," writes Mircea Eliade.[4] Man's city and temple, as well as the entire region he inhabits, are built on celestial models. The act of Creation was a divine act; when man creates, he repeats the divine act, and formalizes the connection through ritual. The sacred city or temple is symbolically the center of the universe, the meeting point of heaven, earth, and hell.[5] The sacred rites of the founding of the city were repeated in regular recurrent festivals, and in its monuments.[6] The founding of cities, even as late as those of the Roman Empire, was a matter of myth and ritual to which practical concerns were completely subordinated.[7] "The city had to be founded by a hero," Rykwert says, and the "hero-founder had to be buried at the heart of the city; only the tomb of the hero-founder could guarantee that the city lived."[8] The distance from this rite of the early city to Pushkin's vivified statue in *The Bronze Horseman* is not as great as one might at first suppose.

Underlying the cosmogony of the founding of the ancient city is the idea that the city of necessity represents a separation from the world of nature, the imposition of man's will on a natural order created by a divinity.[9] This would account for the importance of ritual in the founding of the city. The founding as an act of interference in the divine order also involves a sense of guilt. This guilt might be connected with the curious myth that so many ancient cities were founded by murderers. In Genesis, the first city-founder is Cain; Romulus was also a fratricide founder, and Theseus a parricide founder.[10] In addition to their public names, cities were also given secret names, presumably the name of the protecting deity. Pliny reports that a magistrate was executed for revealing the secret name of Rome.[11] When a city was destroyed, it had to be extirpated ritually as well as physically, reversing the process of founding;[12] it was, after all, the sacred axis of the universe which had to be deconsecrated.

Ellul has a fascinating passage on the word-complex associated with "city" in ancient Hebrew. The word most commonly used for "city" also meant "enemy," and related words for "city" carried as well the meanings of watching angel, vengeance, and terror.[13] These discordant associations are not so surprising for a nomadic people who, until fairly late in their history, did not settle in cities like their neighbors (or enemies).

Against this background it does not surprise us to learn that the recording of history began with the city. Fustel de Coulanges states that "ancient history was sacred and local history. It began with the foundation of the city, because everything prior to that was of no interest."[14]

People in the Middle Ages were familiar with the ancient traditions of planning and founding cities,[15] and of course with the Bible; so there has been from ancient times a historical mechanism for transmitting the concept of the city as an ambivalent image of pride and guilt, although this does not seem by itself to account for the deep-rootedness of the city in the human imagination. It is not possible to determine whether this depth is primarily due to historical transmission, or to the Freudian or Jungian hypotheses of a collective unconscious, possibly (as I shall argue in the last chapter) to man's instinctive responses to his spatial environment, or to some combination of these and other factors. On the level of art, as I have suggested in the Preface, Gombrich's concept of schema seems useful as an explanation of the continuity of representation, in this case of the city. But how attitudes are transmitted on the level of cognition remains a problem. Some authorities reject the idea of continuity in the archetype of the city; Rykwert argues that the modern inhabitant of a city is not aware of its past,[16] and James Mellaart claims that all generalizations about ancient cities are false because there are too many individual differences among them.[17] But these objections seem too literal. The sight of an old church or monument *means* "past" to an observer in the present, and Mellaart neglects, in favor of individual examples, the fact that "city" is a concept.

This book is interested in the response of the human imagination to the phenomenon of "city." From the beginning the image of the city served as the nexus of many things, all characterized by strongly ambivalent feelings: presumption (Babel), corruption (Babylon), perversion (Sodom and Gomorrah), power (Rome), destruction (Troy, Carthage), death, the plague (the City of Dis), and revelation (the heavenly Jerusalem). In Christian thought, the city came to represent both Heaven and Hell. Significantly, the early cities of the epics and the Bible have retained their metaphorical force throughout Western history, as if they stood for certain constants of feeling. Thus Proust could make an important metaphorical point by calling one of the volumes of *In Search of Lost Time* "Sodom and Gomorrah." Several centuries earlier, in 1667, John Dryden had had the inspired idea of dedicating his poem "Annus Mirabilis: The Year of Wonders 1666" to "the Metropolis of Great Britain, the most renowned and late flourishing City of London." Noting in his dedication that he is perhaps the first person to dedicate a poem to a city, Dryden celebrates London for having survived a war, a plague, and a devastating fire: "You, who are to stand a wonder to all Years and Ages, and who have built yourselves an Immortal Monument on your own Ruins. You are now a *Phoenix* in her ashes, and, as far as Humanity can approach, a great Emblem of the suffering Deity."[18]

The city has often been celebrated as the place where the pulse of life is most strongly felt. Samuel Johnson, although well acquainted with adversity in London, never tired of praising the city in poetry, essays, and conversation. His famous epigram is a paradigm of the city's vitality: "When a man is tired of London, he is tired of life."

In modern times the real cities of Western Europe and America have generally tended to be associated with the evils of human nature; ideal cities, on the model of Revelation, have been put off to some vague future time, as in Blake's vow to build Jerusalem in England's green and pleasant land, or the alabaster cities of "America the Beautiful," which gleam (rather curiously) "undimmed by human tears."

The double view of the real city and the mythic city is not so mysterious as might first appear, for all myths are attempts to explain realities. Most basic myths are, however, attempts to account for occurrences of nature. The myth of the city must rationalize an object built by man which, because of its size and concentration of ritual and power (religious, governmental, military, financial) has displaced nature in the natural world.[19]

The myth of the city as corruption, the myth of the city as perfection: This bifocal vision of Western culture is still very much with us. Indeed, the image of the city stands as the great reification of ambivalence, embodying a complex of contradictory forces in both the individual and the collective Western minds. The idea of the city seems to trigger conflicting impulses, positive and negative, conscious and unconscious. At a very deep level, the city seems to express our culture's restless dream about its inner conflicts and its inability to resolve them. On a more conscious level, this ambivalence expresses itself in mixed feelings of pride, guilt, love, fear, and hate toward the city. The fascination people have always felt at the destruction of a city may be partly an expression of satisfaction at the destruction of an emblem of irresolvable conflict.

If one of the writer's functions is to give voice to aspects of culture which are fragmentary perceptions, or preconscious or perhaps even unconscious feelings in the mind of the citizen, then the city is one of the most important metaphors at his command. Technically, the city is an ideal mechanism for the writer, especially the novelist; it enables him to bring together in a plausible network extremely diverse characters, situations, and actions. But this should not mislead us, as readers, into dismissing it as a mere contrivance. The image of the city is a figure with profound tones and overtones, a presence and not simply a setting. This emerges, for instance, in the peculiar opening pages of *Moby-Dick*, in which Ishmael and the city dwellers of Manhattan are drawn magnetically to the edge of the water, yearning outward from their city existence—which itself is presented in strongly negative terms. *Moby-Dick* is not a "city novel," and yet it begins with the image of the city. This opening passage, which arouses resonances in the characters and the reader, stands in a long tradition of the city as a figure for ambivalence in literature.

These conflicting resonances of the image are reinforced by a writer's and reader's own experiences of city life, whether real or imagined. What exactly does happen when one experiences a city in real life? The question itself makes us realize the complexity of the problems facing anthropologist, sociologist, writer, and critic. The basic problem is how to reduce a cacophony of impressions to some kind of harmony. Kevin Lynch has tried to categorize some aspects of this problem as far as empirical response is concerned.[20] The inhabitant or visitor basically experiences the city as a labyrinth, although one with which he may be familiar. He cannot see the whole of a labyrinth at once, except from above, when it becomes a map. Therefore his impressions of it at street level at any given moment will be fragmentary and limited: rooms, buildings, streets. These impressions are primarily visual, but involve the other senses as well, together with a crowd of memories and associations. The impressions a real city makes on an observer are thus both complex and composite in a purely physical sense, even without taking into account his or his culture's pre-existing attitudes. "Observer" is a slightly awkward term to use here since it indicates a person who is, with some awareness, looking at the city from a detached viewpoint. "Observer" applies better to the writer and the narrator than to the citizen. In daily life most urbanites go about in the city concentrating on their immediate business; they swim in the urban ocean without being particularly aware of it. Susanne Langer may call architecture "the total environment made visible," but this remark would certainly nonplus Leopold Bloom.

There is a paradox in this entire situation. The city is, on

9

the one hand, incomprehensible to its inhabitants; as a whole "it is inaccessible to the imagination unless it can be reduced and simplified."[21] But on the other hand, "any individual citizen, by virtue of his particular choices of alternatives for action and experience, will need a vocabulary to express what he imagines the entire city to be."[22]

Literature is an ordering of life, and Blanche Gelfant has suggested a useful deductive framework which shows how it does this. She sees city novels as falling into one of three patterns: the "portrait" type, which reveals the city only through the struggles of an individual protagonist; the "synoptic" novel, in which the city itself rather than an individual character functions as hero, and in which the author emphasizes the multiplicity of city experience; and the "ecological" type, "which focuses upon one small spatial unit such as a neighborhood or city block and explores in detail the manner of life identified with this place."[23]

All three types provide the necessary reduction and simplification by subtly imposing a preliminary ordering on the reader's perception of the word-city. Although the reader may consider the city as it appears in the novel to be a collection of random elements, the writer's choice of perspective has already provided channels for communicating a specific point of view.

Many writers for whom the image of the city is important have been urban journalists and dedicated *flâneurs*, saunterers through the streets of real cities who have paid careful attention to their impressions. Balzac, Dickens, Poe, Baudelaire, Whitman, Dostoevsky, and Zola all fit this mold exactly. But even writers who don't share with the others the peculiar and difficult problem of transposing the urban scene from personal impression to literature. For there is a gulf between the living experience of a real city and the word-city of a poem or novel. How does one make printed statements, ink on paper, into "London," "New York," or "Rome," aside from the associations evoked by the names themselves? Even the sociologist and the urban historian, whose primary obligation is fidelity to empirical reality rather than to the imagination, must, as we say, "reduce" the city to words; for them, as well as for creative writers, the process is one of metaphorization. The sociologist and historian would ideally like to establish identity between the sign and its meaning; the writer calls attention to the separation between them.

This act of reduction brings up another dimension of the problem. A writer does not speak to us directly from his experience, but through language and through the rhetorical conventions of literary forms. These cultural artifacts are historically determined; a writer can express himself and be understood by his readers only by using the literary conventions, vocabulary, and imagery available to him at his particular cultural moment. He may extend them, but displaces them only at the risk of incomprehensibility (Blake's Prophetic Books come to mind). Thus Cedric Whitman writes that "it is idle to ask whether Homer ever saw Troy with his own eyes. Whether he saw it or not, he would have had to describe it in old formulae in any case. Hence what he actually tells us about Troy could have been said of almost any Bronze Age city."[24] Ernst Robert Curtius notes that the rules for poems in praise of cities and countries in the Middle Ages had been worked out in detail by late Roman theory: "The site had first to be treated, then the other excellencies of the city, and not least its significance in respect to the cultivation of the arts and sciences. In the Middle Ages this last topos is given an ecclesiastical turn. The greatest glory of a city now lies in its martyrs (and their relics), its saints, princes of the church, and theologians."[25] In modern literature, the exhaustive examination of Paris as a literary image by Pierre Citron and the sensitive study of London and rural England as metaphors by Raymond Williams give a sobering idea of how deeply a writer's talent is rooted in cultural patterns, and the extent

11

to which his literary vocabulary is actually a received vocabulary.[26]

From the sociological point of view, the individual citizen, according to Wohl and Strauss, is involved "in a continual quest for the essence of his urban experience and for ways to express it. The language used, however, is a formal one. A fairly limited range of linguistic conventions has come into use whose formality is shaped by the fact that the form of the rhetorical devices employed does not depend on their content; their set phrasing is hospitable to any and all substantive statements about a city's qualities."[27] They conclude: "It seems safe to say that without the resources of rhetoric the city-dweller could have no verbal representations of his own or any other city."[28]

So the process by which the writer evokes the city appears to parallel the process by which the citizen seeks to encompass his experience of it. The writer's task is both to evoke and to organize many kinds and levels of response in the reader. It is not the artist who dreams, says Kenneth Burke, but rather the audience, "while the artist oversees the conditions which determine this dream."[29] In this process of overseeing it is clear that the city evoked in words, especially in a fictional text, is toponymical rather than topographical. The name of the city and whatever physical features are labeled function within the relational context of the work; their reference to the real city outside the text may appear to be direct, but is actually indirect. One test of this is the coherence of the word-city to readers who are not the author's contemporaries or countrymen. Raskolnikov's walks through the streets of St. Petersburg in *Crime and Punishment* can be mapped, and would evoke certain associations in readers of Dostoevsky's time and place, but Dostoevsky evokes a thematically coherent city in the text itself, which makes sense a century later to readers in other countries. There are writers who do not sufficiently generalize the city in this way; for example, it is very difficult for a reader to follow Heimito von Doderer's Vienna novels without a thorough topographical and social knowledge of Vienna. Thus, however artfully the word-city may be decked out with the trimmings of a real one, they are parallel or analogous rather than identical: Dickens' London and London, England, are located in two different countries.

Writers seem to pay careful attention to this difference between reality and image. For instance, though Flaubert, Hugo, Balzac, and Dickens have been praised for the realistic urban descriptions in their novels, close examination shows that they typically create in their fictions the Paris or London of a time considerably before the actual time of writing. Through the use of the conventions governing verb tenses in narration, they give the impression of describing a present scene when they are actually inventing the picture of a past one. It is as if, by displacing the city backward in time in this fashion, they wished to insure its metaphorization, to place it as firmly as possible in the realm of the imaginary while at the same time presenting it as a "reality." The result of this procedure is not the evocation of a historically past city but a palimpsestic impression, which results in a tension between the city as past and the city as present.

To point out the discontinuity between the empirical city and its fictional counterpart is not to suggest that in using this image the writer has in mind a secret, coded meaning which the reader is challenged to decipher. That would make the city too literally symbolic, when actually it seems to function primarily as both an emblem and an archetype. As such it has more various and more diffuse associations and resonances than a symbol can generally encompass. However the city-image may function, it always brings into the text a power of its own; it might be more accurate to say that a writer harnesses this image rather than that he creates it. "The poet does not confer the past of his image upon me," Bachelard writes, "and yet his image immediately takes root in me."

13

Bachelard notes in the same work that "great images have both a history and a prehistory; they are always a blend of memory and legend. . . . Every great image has an unfathomable oneiric depth to which the personal past adds special color." And in becoming assimilated into the consciousness of the reader, the image "has touched the depths before it stirs the surface."[30]

Whatever the variety of associations this word conjures up, it has one irreducible core. "City" is, by any definition, a social image. Throughout history, and literary history, it has chiefly represented the idea of community, whatever values might be attached to it in any particular context. For religion, philosophy, and literature from the time of the Greeks and the Old Testament, the image of the city was the image of a community, whether positive or negative. But then this idea began to shift its ground. "From the Renaissance onwards," writes Ian Watt, "there was a growing tendency for individual experience to replace collective tradition as the ultimate arbiter of reality."[31] The modern form of realism began with the idea that the individual could discover the truth through his senses, and this concept led to the rise of the novel as a literary form. Whereas earlier literary forms had been characterized by making "conformity to traditional practice the major test of truth," the primary criterion of the novel was "truth to individual experience."[32] Thus the plot of the novel "had to be acted out by particular people in particular circumstances, rather than, as had been common in the past, by general human types against a background primarily determined by the appropriate literary convention."[33]

One of the favorite devices of the eighteenth-century novel was to play off an individual outcast against an urban community of shared values. Moll Flanders is a criminal operating on the community of bourgeois mercantile London (although her religious conversion reunites her with society on a higher level for both). The primacy of the community's shared values is still operating in Balzac, if with less conviction; Balzac's heroes and heroines are typically outsiders, like Rastignac or Lucien Chardon, whose goal in life is to get to the top of the shaky heap. But the presence of Vautrin in Balzac's world shows how the idea of an urban community as a community of shared values was losing its force. Vautrin strikes a different note from Moll Flanders'; her criminality defines the boundaries of an integral community she is operating against, his subverts the whole idea of a community which Balzac presents as essentially corrupt to begin with. And throughout the nineteenth century we find that the isolation of the individual rather than the cohesion of urban society becomes increasingly the focus of the image of the city. Dickens' extreme emphasis on portraying urban eccentrics is an indirect witness to this shift; Baudelaire's neurotic poet and Dostoevsky's underground man and Raskolnikov are direct statements of it.[34]

This new emphasis on the isolated individual applies not only to characters in novels, but also to the stress which nineteenth- and twentieth-century writers and critics put on the concept of the narrator (or, in poetry, the speaker), whose individualized point of view is the lens through which the reader views the world of the work. Of special interest is the way in which character or narrator typically presents himself alone against the city, an isolated individual consciousness observing the urban community. It is this stance which makes Hawthorne's "paved solitude" a paradigm for the city in modern literature.

Henry James' *The American Scene* is a work of non-fiction written by a novelist. Many of its passages combine the personal reactions of a sharp-witted observer of cities with the boldness of the novelist's invention. James frequently sees the city as casting back an image of truth at a self-deluded character, as Paris does to Strether in *The Ambassadors*; in *The American Scene* the image is cast back at James himself. Sum-

15

ming up his impression at seeing New York again after an absence of a quarter-century, James writes that "the sky-scrapers and the league-long bridges, present and to come, marked the point where the age . . . had come out. That in itself was nothing—ages do come out, as a matter of course, so far from where they have gone in. But it had done so, the latter half of the nineteenth century, in one's own more or less immediate presence; the difference, from pole to pole, was so vivid and concrete that no single shade of any one of its aspects was lost. This impact of the whole condensed past at once produced a horrible, hateful sense of personal antiquity."[35]

In this complicated reaction to the city James makes the physical city an organism like himself, whose changes and rhythms in both time and space are, however, on a different scale and rhythm from his own. It is this discrepancy which reminds him so abruptly of his "personal antiquity" when suddenly faced with "the whole condensed past." The overall impression of the physical city to one who observes it, as James does here, is of buildings and streets deposited in sedimentary fashion over a long period, and implying a future ("present and to come").

Robert Musil also makes witty use of this slow rhythm of accretion separating a city's growth from the faster rhythm of an individual life. In describing the grounds and house in Vienna which belong to Ulrich, the man without qualities, the narrator evokes "a garden, partly still preserved from the eighteenth, or even the seventeenth, century; and if one strolled past its wrought-iron fence, one glimpsed something like a short-winged little castle, a hunting lodge or pleasure palace from bygone times. Precisely speaking, its cellar vaults were from the seventeenth century, the garden and the main floor bore the appearance of the eighteenth century, the façade had been renovated and rather spoiled in the nineteenth century. The whole made, in short, a rather blurred

16

impression, like superimposed photographic images; but of such a kind that one invariably stopped and said 'Ah!' "[36] This description of the past frozen as an architectural jumble in the present is a spatial representation of a long time-scale. This contrasts with the shorter time-scale of Ulrich, who is introduced immediately after this description of his house.

This contrast can, of course, work in the opposite way: instead of long, slow accretion the architectural representation of the past can disappear very quickly, through acts of war, nature, or economics. In this case the time-span of the individual would be longer than that of the urban environment. Baudelaire seems to have been the first writer who systematically exploited these syncopated rhythms as a way of indicating the estrangement of the individual from the city. For if in earlier times the city had been predominantly an image of fixed relationships and fixed elements, during the nineteenth century it became a primary image of flux, of dislocation rather than location. In our own time the word-city seems to be less a place than a negative atmosphere full of crackling static within which disembodied voices speak.

However, the image of the city seen historically only partly explains its fascination. At a deeper level, as I have indicated, the widely varying historical cities of Western culture are the same city, a powerful archetype-emblem representing deep-rooted social and psychological constants. For this reason history and cultural psychology are intimately linked in any study of the literary city. An arresting example of this symbiotic relationship occurs in an essay which lies on the borderline between science and poetry, Freud's *Civilization and Its Discontents*.[37] The figure of the city was a strong emblematic magnet for Freud; he is elsewhere drawn to Pompeii and London. In this late essay he uses the city of Rome as an incidental but profound and curious analogy. In seeking to illustrate the point that the primitive part of the brain still survives in the brain of modern man, Freud turns to the city

17

as illustration. He first refers to "the history of the Eternal City," which he only then goes on to identify as Rome. It is as if this common tag for Rome ("the Eternal City") were important for him in a literal sense, standing for something which has survived through time basically unchanged; this is indeed the argument Freud goes on to develop. Traces of early stages in the development of the brain still survive in the modern brain, he argues, in the same way that traces of the history and pre-history of the "Eternal City" still survive in present-day Rome.[38]

In a remarkable flight of the imagination, bordering on reverie, Freud asks his reader to visualize a surrealistic picture: wherever we might look in contemporary Rome we would see, simultaneously with a present building and occupying the same space, all the earlier structures which had ever stood on that one spot. As if rousing himself, he then goes on to reject his own analogy. One cannot, he says, represent mental life in pictorial (that is, spatial) terms.[39] But the analogy has been made, and it has been made with the evocative power we might expect from a poet. Indeed, the comparison has so much force that Freud himself felt it necessary to comment further on it. As he continues his argument, he returns to the strictures of scientific discourse, but he notes in one of those asides which seem to hang in the air long after they are spoken: "The question may be raised why we chose precisely the past of a *city* to compare with the past of the mind."[40] It is a question he does not really answer.

The surrealistic impression of Freud's metaphor results from the superimposition of spatial forms on a temporal sequence, and from the juxtaposition of one particular historical city, Rome, and the archetype of the "eternal city." This process resembles Musil's metaphor of the superimposition of historical styles in Ulrich's house, except that Freud has added psychology to history more overtly; it is also reminiscent of the early pattern according to which the city had to be founded on a ritualized mythic basis.

Freud's subject in this passage is the mind, not the city. He uses the city only as an illustration, and yet, for both author and reader, the image seems to have resonances which have nothing to do with the context. His point would be quite clear without any image at all. Freud's life provides an interesting clue to the power of this particular figure. His biographer Ernest Jones points out that Freud attached great importance to Rome, and that this city had great emotional significance for him. Jones concludes that for Freud "Rome contained two entities, one loved, the other feared and hated";[41] in other words, that it was for him a perfect emblem of ambivalence.

It would, however, be a mistake to stop with this personal explanation. There seems to have been in Freud's thinking an association between civilization (*Kultur*) as the highest product of the human mind, and the city as the densest—and at the same time the most rarefied—distillation of civilization. This association is unstated, but it does not appear to have been entirely unconscious on Freud's part, since he himself wonders in print why he chose a city as a metaphor. (This time he writes "a city" rather than "the Eternal City" or "Rome.") One might speculate further that the choice of Rome is both appropriate and necessary for his comparison, for Rome presents the observer with the image of a living city in the present superimposed on the impressive ruins of a ghostly past. Rome is a living community, but its life rests on the many layers of the dead, who have left visible and grandiose reminders of their former presence. Rome is also, of course, one of the main foundation stones of our culture, the *locus classicus* of Western civilization: "at once the Paradise, / The grave, the city, and the wilderness," Shelley called it in "Adonais," the twin oxymorons underlining its ambivalence for Keats, Shelley himself, and European culture.

In contrast to Rome, present and past, one has only to

imagine a totally dead city of archeological ruins, which has no present, or a totally modern city which has no past or which has obliterated its past. Neither would have suited *Civilization and Its Discontents*. The eternal city had to be Rome, because the primary emphasis in Freud's image is on the city as a continuum between the monumental past and his own present, between the dead and the living. Since Freud's subject is man's mind, perceived as a continuum still containing traces of its collective past, we can see why his metaphor probably shaped itself the way it did. (Freud's idea of the city as a continuum was picked up and somewhat flattened by Lewis Mumford, for instance when Mumford notes that "the modern city itself, for all its steel and glass, is still essentially an earth-bound Stone Age structure.")[42]

It is curious that Freud draws back from his parallel between mind and city while letting it stand. A logical response, especially from such a careful stylist as Freud, would normally be to remove from the text a passage which the writer considered inappropriate. That he did not do so makes the process of stating the image, and then rejecting it, part of his argument. The resulting palimpsest reinforces the idea of ambivalence toward culture which lies at the heart of this essay.

Later in *Civilization and Its Discontents* the city reappears in an arresting image which links it to a sense of guilt: "The tension between the harsh super-ego and the ego that is subjected to it, is called by us the sense of guilt; it expresses itself as a need for punishment. Civilization, therefore, obtains mastery over the individual's dangerous desire for aggression by weakening and disarming it and by setting up an agency within him to watch over it, like a garrison in a conquered city."[43] At the end of the essay the suggestiveness of the city image is considerably deepened, in more generalized terms. In discussing the struggle between Eros and the death instinct, and the sense of guilt to which this struggle gives rise, Freud speaks of the transfer of this guilt feeling from the family to the community. Civilization, he argues, is a necessary course of development from the family to humanity as a whole. But this development involves the transfer of family conflict and its attendant sense of guilt to the wider community. Freud carries this provocative idea rather far in asserting that the community, like the individual, evolves a superego "under whose influence cultural development proceeds." This identification—it is by now far more than an analogy—carries with it the vital corollary that, if the development of civilization does indeed follow the same processes as the development of the individual, "may we not be justified in reaching the conclusion that, under the influence of cultural urges, some civilizations, or some epochs of civilization—possibly the whole of mankind—have become neurotic?"[44]

If we were now to say, on the basis of Freud's argument, that the city occupies a special place as the most intense locus of culture within a given civilization, then we could apply to the city Freud's points about conflict, guilt, the function of the superego, and neurosis as factors in the development of civilization. Freud's line of thought reflects ambivalence: the dark shadows of conflict, aggression, and guilt are an integral part of civilization, which is man's greatest achievement and the ultimate container and transmitter of his highest values.

Lewis Mumford again caught the urban implications of Freud's argument. "No matter how many valuable functions the city has furthered," Mumford writes, "it has also served, throughout most of its history, as a container of organized violence and a transmitter of war." In the walled city, Mumford continues, "the division of labor and castes, pushed to the extreme, normalized schizophrenia; while the compulsive repetitious labor imposed on a large part of the urban population under slavery, reproduced the structure of a compulsion neurosis. Thus the ancient city, in its very constitution, tended to transmit a collective personality structure whose more extreme manifestations are now recognized in individuals as pathological."[45]

Freud's insights and Mumford's application of them are further evidence that the city as an image in culture (and consequently in literature) is not a superficial matter, but has, on the contrary, profound associations for both writers and readers. Some sociological writing on the city overlooks these associations. Thus Morton and Lucia White assert that America's "most celebrated thinkers have expressed different degrees of ambivalence and animosity toward the city. . . . We have no persistent or pervasive tradition of romantic attachment to the city in our literature or in our philosophy, nothing like the Greek attachment to the *polis* or the French writer's affection for Paris. And this confirms the frequently advanced thesis that the American intellectual has been alienated from the society in which he has lived, that he has been typically in revolt against it. For while our society became more and more urban throughout the nineteenth century, the literary tendency to denigrate the city hardly declined; if anything, its intensity increased. One of the most typical elements in our national life, the growing city, became the bête noire of our most distinguished intellectuals rather than their favorite."[46] This argument does not go far enough. If the Whites had looked more deeply into the ambivalence reflected in the city, they would have found that it is characteristic of far more than nineteenth-century American society. It has been a striking phenomenon of Western culture since ancient times.

The word-city, then, leads a double life, evoking deep-rooted archetypal associations while its surface features reflect changing attitudes and values. Viewers of medieval paintings and woodcuts depicting cities are struck by the fact that a representation of Jerusalem, for instance, is that of a medieval city. E. H. Gombrich refers to the illustrations in Hartmann Schedel's "Nuremberg Chronicle," in which the identical

22

woodcut of a medieval city recurs with different captions as Damascus, Ferrara, Milan, and Mantua; all that these pictures were expected to do, Gombrich writes, "was to bring home to the reader that these names stood for cities."[47] What was to be depicted was the idea, not the concrete individualized form. Gombrich calls this "the principle of the adapted stereotype,"[48] in which the illustrator depicts an inner stereotype derived from the current culture, rather than an objective rendering of a real city.

Such an adapted stereotype occurs in Hawthorne's "The Gray Champion." In this story from *Twice-Told Tales* the city is located in the past rather than the present: Hawthorne is ostensibly writing about Boston during the colonial period. But the fine icy chill of the passage which serves as epigraph to this chapter belongs to the writer of 1837, not to the screen Boston of "1689." This single use of the image of the city contains many layers of meaning: "The crowd had rolled back and were now huddled together nearly at the extremity of the street, while the soldiers had advanced no more than a third of its length. The intervening space was empty—a paved solitude between lofty edifices, which threw almost a twilight shadow over it."

The whole weight of these two sentences falls on the emptiness of something which should be full, and which is made to serve a function opposite to the one for which it was intended. A city street lined with buildings was designed to be, literally and figuratively, an avenue of communication of all kinds. It is an emblem of both *civitas* and *communitas*. Hawthorne, with great care and deliberation, in this image turns this basic assumption of positive space into a negative one. He empties the street and uses it instead as a brooding figure which separates two hostile masses, the people at one end and the soldiers advancing toward them from the other. The street is filled with a tense emptiness. The two groups have lost their individuality; they are compressed into two masses, one "huddled," one composed of the uniformity of soldiers. Since the street is denied its natural functions, the buildings which line it seem to come alive with a threatening presence of their own; as "lofty edifices" they seem higher and more stern than mere buildings. In this negative space the soldiers represent the instinct of aggression, the cowed populace the instincts of hatred and fear. The empty space of the street shows forcefully how community, civilization in the form of the city, is blotted out by the breaking through of these primitive instincts. At this point in his story, Hawthorne is articulating the disruption of civilization, embodied in the physical form of the city, by the forces of aggression and fear which underlie it and which civilization must constantly seek to control.

It is as a result of the eruption of these dark instincts that the street's normal function is destroyed and it becomes a "paved solitude." "Paved" implies all the purposefulness of modern city life: business, activity, communication. "Solitude" is the denial of all this. A grand word of Miltonic and Wordsworthian ring in English, "solitude" is both existential and topographic. It refers both to the aloneness of an individual and to a lonely place, generally rural. "Solitude" is also an ambiguous term: it can mean a place of either alienation or refuge. In *The Machine in the Garden*, Leo Marx quotes passages from many nineteenth-century American writers in which "solitude" is used as a synonym for "desert."[49] It represents a wilderness as opposed to the idealized landscape of the middle distance, the pastoral landscape, whose model is the harmony of men and nature; the model for solitude is isolation. "Solitude" is an abstract word as well as a dramatic one; it does not bring to mind any specific locality with characteristic features, but rather seems to express the state of mind of an observer contemplating an unpeopled landscape.

Hawthorne brings this state of mind to the city. It is the observing narrator and not the characters involved for whom the tension of this scene is expressed in the verbal tension of combining "paved" with "solitude." The characters in this passage are not included in the solitude, which refers to the empty street-space separating the two groups. By raising the simple concept of "intervening space" to the complicated and clashing ambivalence of "paved solitude," Hawthorne brings the city into the action of his story. The "lofty edifices," buildings deprived of their function as the street is deprived of its function, emerge as inscrutable, shadow-casting monuments rather than as structures serving a living society. ("Lofty edifices" is not descriptive but a purely verbal projection of a heightened mood, here one of menace. There were no high buildings in Boston in either 1689 or 1837.) Mumford's characterization of the modern city as "still essentially an earthbound Stone Age structure" again comes to mind; Hawthorne is throwing his reader back from 1837 to well before "1689," to the archetypal ambivalence of the city as the home of man.

The metaphorical application of solitude to the city was by no means limited to America in the nineteenth century. Baudelaire, for example, was fond in his poetry of playing off the solitude of the observing poet against the city as a collective scene. Just how conscious and deliberate this was on his part can be seen in a section of *The Spleen of Paris* called "Crowds":

Multitude, solitude: equal and convertible terms for the active and fecund poet. He who does not know how to people his solitude will not know either how to be alone in a bustling crowd.

The poet enjoys the incomparable privilege of being able as he likes to be himself and others. Like those wandering souls which search for a body, he can enter every person whenever he wants. For him alone, everything is empty. . . .

The solitary and pensive walker draws from this universal communion a singular sense of intoxication.[50]

25

Ever the Latin linguist, Baudelaire begins by playing on the antiphonal contrast between "multitude" and "solitude," manyness and oneness, which he proceeds to equate. Using the terms to mean "togetherness" and "isolation," he throws them in the air and plays with them like a juggler. The isolated poet can through his imagination be the many as well as the one; he can be both "solitary and pensive" and partake at the same time of the "universal communion." (Baudelaire's use of the religious term is interesting, underlining as it does the integration of the individual into the sharing group in a ceremony of reconciliation.) As a poet, the individual must be isolated from the group in order to create, but through his imagination, and his poetry, he can join it. This sovereign freedom understandably produces in the poet "a singular sense of intoxication."

However, this intoxication is indeed singular. The underlying tone of this passage is not that of the playful equation of opposites, but the expression of a splenetic solitude; as Walter Benjamin has pointed out, Baudelaire's attitude toward the city is predominantly negative.[51] Henri Lefebvre, though not discussing Baudelaire specifically, has perhaps pinpointed this quirkiness more exactly in a thought about the extreme ambivalence of modern society. This ambivalence expresses itself in two contradictory obsessions, integrating and disintegrating. Lefebvre sees one of these obsessions, the compulsive need to integrate and be integrated, as a response to the other, the disintegration of the idea of community.[52]

Clashing contradictions: perhaps the central fascination of the city, both real and fictional, is that it embodies man's contradictory feelings—pride, love, anxiety, and hatred—toward the civilization he has created and the culture to which he belongs.

The Static City

The city lies foursquare, its length the same as its
breadth. . . . The wall was built of jasper, while the
city was pure gold, clear as glass.

—*Revelation*

Over the course of the nineteenth century the representation
of the city in European and American literature gradually
underwent two important shifts in emphasis. One was a
movement from stasis to flux: The institutions of the city, its
physical monuments and social classes, were portrayed less
and less as elements perceptually fixed in relation to each
other and more and more as a succession of fluid and unpredictable juxtapositions. The other shift was from the urban
community as a pattern of the whole (which could be negative
as well as positive, as in Balzac) to the isolation of the individual within it. These changes occur both singly and in combination, and overlap chronologically as well. As a way of
apprehending them, this chapter will focus on the static city
and the next chapter on the city in flux from the eighteenth
to the early twentieth century. Different works by the same
author will in some cases be used in each chapter, according
to their primary emphasis.

The city as a static, perceptually fixed image seems to reflect a generalized rhetorical stereotype surviving from the time before individualized description of the city displaced the fixed topos. Thus Wordsworth's sonnet, "Composed upon Westminster Bridge, September 3, 1802," presents the city as a type, whose most specific features ("ships, towers, domes, theatres, and temples") are emblems of the city in general as seat of secular, religious, commercial, and artistic power. Were it not for the title, nothing in the poem would identify this city as London or the date as the beginning of the nineteenth century.[1]

Ambivalence is as involved in the static representation of the city as it is in the flowing perspective.

Composed upon Westminster Bridge
September 3, 1802

Earth has not anything to show more fair:
Dull would he be of soul who could pass by
A sight so touching in its majesty:
This City now doth, like a garment, wear
The beauty of the morning; silent, bare,
Ships, towers, domes, theatres, and temples lie
Open unto the fields, and to the sky;
All bright and glittering in the smokeless air.
Never did sun more beautifully steep
In his first splendour, valley, rock, or hill;
Ne'er saw I, never felt, a calm so deep!
The river glideth at his own sweet will:
Dear God! the very houses seem asleep;
And all that mighty heart is lying still!

Wordsworth is here looking at the city from outside. He is ostensibly seeing what we artlessly call in everyday language "the heart of the city" from a point of suspension in both space and time above the water of the river. The poet sees the city as a "mighty heart" (presumably to England's body), but lying static in sleep. Because the title and subtitle locate the city and the poet so precisely in both time and place, the reader has the impression that Wordsworth is spontaneously transcribing the effect of a striking scene. This was, however, not the case; this poem is a *trompe l'oeil* reconstruction of a fleeting impression. Wordsworth himself noted that the poem was "composed on the roof of a coach, on my way to France." But it appears that he was "passing by" in another sense, for Wordsworth went to France on July 31, 1802, not September 3. The mystery is resolved by his sister, who noted that this sight made a deep impression on him as they left London, but that he did not actually write the poem until a month later—which would account for the date of September 3.[2]

Thus the time and place in which this poem is so prominently anchored are displaced; "upon" is not literal but figurative, and "September 3, 1802" is the date of writing, not the date of the vision. The specific title of this generalized poem about the city is also an illusion. This curious anomaly can be resolved if we regard the city in this poem as an object which crystallizes the poet's emotions rather than as the poem's subject. The subject would be the surge of feeling in the poet in response to the view. Seen in this way, "Composed upon Westminster Bridge, September 3, 1802" would refer to the poet's "moment" rather than the city's, which is clearly identified within the poem as dawn.

Wordsworth bestows his highest praise on this arrested object by comparing it favorably with the country, the world of pastoral nature. The first line of the poem, as well as the later explicit comparison, welcomes the city into the unity of "earth," although the poem treats the city as different in kind from "valley, rock, or hill." One might be tempted to call this sonnet a landscape, in pictorial terms; and yet, for all its idyllic quality, a powerful tide of contradiction runs beneath the static surface.

The fixed points of this city given in the poem are those

representations of commerce, power, art, and religion which have been the hallmarks of the city since ancient times, and they bring into the poem a suggestion of latent mythic power. The majesty of the view does not seem to include "houses," human dwellings, which are mentioned only late and incidentally as part of the scene. The function of these ships and buildings is bustling human activity, organized to serve various social purposes, yet the poet sees them as silent, bare, smokeless, and apparently asleep. His city has no people in it. This city is a "mighty heart," but instead of pumping blood, or life, it is said to be "lying still," the situation of sleep—or death; "mighty heart" and "lying still" almost constitute an oxymoron. It is as if the city, seen in depopulated, death-like repose, has left the world of human activity where it belongs to become another object in the world of nature, like Lucy in the poem "A Slumber did my Spirit Steal."

The poet knows that this city is not dead but asleep. The last line of the poem is a poetic conceit, suggested by his view, real or recollected, of the city at an uncharacteristic time. His choice of this time insures that his vision of the city will be static rather than dynamic.

A half-century before "Westminster Bridge," in a satirical tale called *The World as It Is* (1748), Voltaire had anchored an equivocal attitude toward European civilization in a city which was also fixed and generalized.[3] The city in this story is the image through which a culture is judged and found wanting. It is threatened with destruction for its shortcomings by a supernatural power, but it is not, finally, destroyed.

Voltaire uses his familiar rhetorical device of having an innocent stranger apply common sense to the vanities of Paris. The scene is lightly disguised as the Middle East. Though this kind of substitution was a popular convention of the time, especially with Voltaire, it has the effect of generalizing the city. It is no longer simply Paris, but also the city as the hearth of civilization. The angel Ituriel charges a Scythian, Babouc, with visiting "Persepolis" and reporting on its mores and values. "On your report," the angel tells Babouc, "I will determine whether to correct the city or exterminate it." Both on his journey and in Persepolis, Babouc is struck by the contradictory behavior of the people he sees, who seem equally capable of baseness and sublimity, virtues and crimes. The narrative structure of the tale is dramatic; as Ituriel's threat hangs over the city, Babouc alternately registers disgust at the baseness he observes and surprise at the virtues.

Although Voltaire is not generally considered a mythic thinker, he was fond of using mythic structures. In *The World as It Is*, Babouc witnesses the interment of a corpse in a temple: "What!" Babouc cried, "these people bury their dead in the same places where they adore the Divinity! What! Their temples are paved with corpses! I am no longer surprised at those pestilential diseases which often ravage Persepolis. The putrefaction of the dead and that of so many living assembled and pressed together in the same place is capable of poisoning the entire globe. Ah! What a vile place Persepolis is! Apparently the angels want to destroy it in order to rebuild a finer one, and to people it with inhabitants who are less indecent and who sing better."

Here Voltaire is maneuvering institutional religion into the corner of superstition, but the association of religious worship with respect and care for the dead and their tombs appears to have been one of the essential elements of early cities, and part of the myths underlying later ones.[4]

As Babouc looks around the city, his reactions reflect ambivalence rather than resolution; he sees that Persepolis contains good people as well as idiots. The narrator uses an architectural image for this ambivalence: Babouc "finally suspected that the customs of Persepolis could well be like its buildings, of which some had seemed to him worthy of pity while others had enraptured him with admiration." The physical structure of this city is equated with its culture.

31

The strongest expression of the ambivalence of this city image comes at the end of this castigating tale, which does not provide the judgment one might expect. Something else happens: Babouc is corrupted by the civilized pleasures of the city; he doesn't judge the city, he falls in love with it and excuses its faults. He forgets Ituriel in favor of Téone, a seductive figure who presides over all the pleasures and who possesses all the ideal virtues. Babouc is in a quandary about what to report to Ituriel, and finally hits upon the idea of having made "by the best founder of the city a small statue composed of all the metals, earths, and stones the most precious and most vile; he carried it to Ituriel: 'Will you,' he asked him, 'break this pretty statue because it is not all gold and diamonds?' " Ituriel gets the message: "He resolved not even to think of correcting Persepolis but to let the world go on the way it was, 'for,' he said, 'if everything isn't good, at least it's passable.' " In the edition of 1756 Voltaire underlined this conclusion, with its oblique nod to Leibnitz, by adding a somewhat immoral moral: "Thus Persepolis was allowed to go on existing, and Babouc was far from complaining like Jonah, who was vexed because Nineveh was not destroyed. But when one has been in the belly of a whale for three days one is not in as good spirits as when one has been at the opera, at the theater, and dined in good company."

Voltaire's tale is generalized, its city an adapted stereotype. The idea of eighteenth-century Paris, without any specific features, is understood through literary convention as "meant" by the mythical Near Eastern Persepolis. Between Defoe and Balzac, as individual experience became increasingly the test of reality, words in literature came to correspond to specific objects rather than to stereotypes.[5] This process of individuation began in the novel with literary characters: Moll Flanders is a particular individual, but her London is undifferentiated, in spite of Defoe's frequent use of street and place names. In Romantic literature cities, where they occur, are still seen generally, but are usually tied to the particular state of mind or feeling of the author or central character, as in Wordsworth's "Westminster Bridge." It was not really until Balzac that the word-city itself was individualized; this is one of the things we mean when we talk about "realistic description." Mme. Vauquer's boarding house in *Père Goriot* is an exclusively Parisian institution.

But even though individualized description came to replace the stereotype, the representation of the city in literature remained through much of the nineteenth century the verbal rendition of a static perception. During this time the European or American writer was expected to present his readers with a coherently coded word-picture in which people, places, and things bore the same apparent relation to each other as they did in life. The city was conceptualized as a collection of discrete and detailed objects fixed in space, with the characters moving in and among them. These fixed relationships could, on occasion, be stretched into fantasy, but even the fantasies—of which we shall see several examples—are still spatially oriented. The explicitness of this spatial mimesis was probably attuned to the large audience for which serious literature was still written in the nineteenth century; to reach this audience it was necessary to preserve the apparent familiarity of its world.

This kind of spatial mimesis also dictated, to a large extent, the technical means an author could use in constructing his image of the city. The most important of these was his choice of spatial viewpoint. Here there were three main possibilities: The narrator or narrative could present the city from above, from street level, or from below. Occasionally—an extension of the horizontal view—the city would be seen as a whole from a point outside it, as in Wordsworth's "Westminster Bridge." In longer works such as novels, writers had to vary this perspective, but in any single episode it is seen from one fixed narrative viewpoint. The mimetic demands of realistic style also underscored one particular convention: if the word-city is thought of as representing a collection of objects fixed in space, it must be quite literally a "setting." The image could not be fragmented beyond the point at which the reader would become disoriented.

Each of these three narrative viewpoints—from above, from street level, and from below—brought into play different implications and possibilities. One can appreciate the importance of this choice by trying, for instance, to imagine busy Moll Flanders looking down on London from above or, in the opposite case, Balzac's ubiquitous narrator trying to evoke Parisian society from the sewers under the streets of the French capital.

When a writer looks at the city from above, he is placing himself (or his narrator) and the reader in an attitude of contemplation rather than involvement. The elevated observer is within the city but above it at the same time, removed from the daily life taking place on the streets and within buildings. He can look up at the sky and out at the horizon as well as down at the city itself. This greatly diminishes the city in size and its activity in importance in relation to the emptiness and silence of the spaces around it. From this perspective what is observed must pass throught the filter of the narrating consciousness, whether it is the narrator's or the author's. This reinforces the isolation of the speaking voice, since it is the only "character" in such scenes. And since this superior position involves judgment as well as observation, it can be an analog of the divine as well as of the authorial mind.

If seeing the city from above in prose and poetry involves a process of contemplation, seeing it from street level is to experience it actively. Here one finds oneself in a labyrinth. Sight-lines are limited by corners, crowds and traffic; constant watchfulness is called for. One must both make one's way and be alert for possible dangers, which come in a multitude of forms dear to the novelist and poet. One's course through the city is also labyrinthine, strung on the thread of one's purpose (which produces an element of suspense: Is Odette home? What will happen to Raskolnikov at the police station?). This progress is subject to constant distractions and the consequent need for concentration. Confrontations with friends or enemies are always possible. In operating at street level the writer can call many different strands of psychic energy into play for both his characters and his readers.

Although the city as labyrinth is determined in the static mode (the streets and buildings are fixed and have fixed identities), it is also highly susceptible to chance (in the encounters of people within the fixity). This combination makes the street-level city the modern vehicle for the journey of adventure. Joyce well understood that a latter-day *Odyssey* would have to be urban, and presented from a horizontal view the streets seen as a fixed maze.

The street-level vantage point is the most common in city literature. It is a marvelous vehicle for conveying complexity, as well as being closest to the reader's everyday experience: a fixed place, rich in resonances of all kinds, which offers a setting or atmosphere for action, and which at the same time involves many variables and a high degree of uncertainty. This viewpoint becomes especially interesting when the writer's own psyche is involved in it. I have noted that many nineteenth-century writers were passionate *flâneurs*, musing roamers of the streets. Fascination with the city experienced as a labyrinth was an important element in their lives, and adds an extra aura of intensity to their novels or poems. It is as if early experience of the city had imprinted these authors with its patterns and rhythms, so that when they later chose the city as a literary device they were able to highlight it against a dark and amorphous background. An external factor also played a role: cities in the nineteenth century were exploding in size and population, and it became increasingly difficult to see them as stable and familiar. These rapid changes and the resulting instability were a source of ambivalent attraction to urban writers of the time, like Hugo, Baudelaire, and Dickens; they had some objective basis for looking back to the cities of their youth as more stable than the cities of their adulthood.

In making the jump from their own wanderings through the city to literature, writers discovered that the streets of the city were a mimetic equivalent of the structure and myth of the labyrinth. Whether or not they all were conscious of it, they had found a device which could expand the realistic conventions of a middle-class art to include psychology and myth. Combined with the traditional devices of literary rhetoric, these new possibilities opened many avenues of communication between writers and readers.

The subterranean view of the city is closer to the realms of myth and instinct. To see the city from below is to demonize it. One is "at the roots" in many senses: in the city of the past on which the city of the present is built; in the vaults and sewers which are the cloacal parts of the living city; in the realm of the dead, whose once living bodies underlie the bustle of the present time, and, figuratively, in the world of the unconscious. For instance, the original placement of cemeteries beside cities (expansion of the cities usually engulfs them) is apparently a long-surviving cultural pattern with mythic overtones. Lewis Mumford speculates that the very first cities were indeed cities of the dead, the first streets the rows of graves laid out by nomadic tribes. The nomads returned periodically to visit the grave sites, and eventually settled down beside them, establishing the layout of their communities on the pattern of the cemeteries.[6]

The underground viewpoint also comes close to Freud's analogy between the mind and the city in *Civilization and Its Discontents* and to his suggestion of the existence of a collective unconscious in *Totem and Taboo*. Looked at this way, the underground represents more than the past of the psyche surviving into the present; it would include as well the primitive aspects of the mind itself, the id which "underlies" (as language forces us to say) the ego. The myth of the underworld had been around for a long time in legend and literature before it was overtly connected to the city in terms of catacombs, roots, and sewers; psychology gives us a metaphor to make the connection more meaningful. If the underground is the region of the unconscious "id," the horizontal surface of city streets and the view from above may be taken to represent generally the rational sphere of the "ego" and "superego." (Here, as throughout, I am using Freud's terms figuratively.) The writer who grasped these relationships most arrestingly was Victor Hugo; in *Les Misérables* he presents the subterranean labyrinth of the sewers of Paris as a dark mirror image of the urban labyrinth above, heightening the contrast by emphasizing the sudden adits and exits between them. *Notre Dame* utilizes all three levels.

One of the most absorbing parts of *Les Misérables* is a chase through the sewers of Paris which shows the psychic and mythic forces at work in the nineteenth-century detective novel, the genre to which the basic framework of *Les Misérables* belongs. Hugo's coldly intellectual detective Javert is surely as extreme a representation of "superego" as can be found in literature. Javert's quarry is the god-demon Valjean, who seems to combine the qualities of mythic divinity and "id." Javert pursues him through the labyrinth of the streets, then through the doubled labyrinth of the underworld, the sewers under the streets. Valjean, the god-demon, is encumbered in his flight through the sewers by the burden of the wounded and unconscious bourgeois Marius, whom Valjean is saving/abducting. In passages of air inside the earth, the god-demon is pursued by fire (the torches of the police) through the realm of water (the sewers) which nearly drowns him.

For the context of this chase, Hugo provides one of his customary wide sweeps of the net. The section of *Les*

Misérables which precedes the underground pursuit is called "The Bowels of Leviathan." Hugo does not develop this suggestive metaphor, but begins this section by presenting statistics on the amount of sewage produced by Paris. In the line of nineteenth-century scientizing (in this instance designed, no doubt, to make the unpalatable palatable to his readers), he compares the volume of sewage in Paris with that in other cities, and discusses such arcane matters as the value of human fertilizer in China. Like Balzac and Zola, Hugo casts himself in the role of social scientist: "The social observer must enter these shadows; they form part of his laboratory."[7] This entire part of his novel is devoted to a rhapsody on the science, history, sociology, and poetry of sewer systems; it is an extended essay which lies outside the narrative action of the novel, a disquisition directed without mediation from author to reader. But on the base of this "scientific" presentation the sewers of Hugo's Paris are energized through the chase and infused with mythic force, much as in *Moby-Dick* the final chase rests on the preceding encyclopedia of whaling. The sewers in *Les Misérables* double the streets and avenues of Paris in space in the same way in which Hugo's placing the action of the novel in the past doubles it in time. (The action takes place between 1815 and 1832; the novel was written from 1845 to 1862.) The underground labyrinth is a strong representation of the repressed part of the life of society above ground. Hugo's wide-ranging essay shows that he was fully aware of these ramifications of his image. The sewers represent the primal unconscious underlying modern urban society, and Hugo uses them to link his Paris to cities of the past, and to the idea of the city.

Although it occupies only a small proportion of a long work, this use of the underground viewpoint in *Les Misérables* looms very large in the novel in terms of relative intensity. It is peculiarly reinforced at the novel's close when the god-demon is buried *above* the city: *Les Misérables* ends, like Balzac's *Père*

Goriot, in the cemetery of Père Lachaise on a hill overlooking Paris. Valjean is buried there in the common pauper's grave, "far from the elegant quarter of this city of tombs."[8]

An even more arresting example of this use of spatial perspective occurs in Zola's *Germinal*. In this instance the city is not a setting but an isolated spatial metaphor for a subterranean catastrophe. The terrorist Souvarine has sabotaged the shaft of a coal mine, causing the waters of an underground lake to flood the mine. Negrel, the supervisor, is being lowered cautiously down the shaft to find out what is happening. The narrator of this realistic, mythicizing novel reports that "the waters of the Torrent, the underground sea with its mysterious storms and wrecks, were gushing forth as through a weir. He went lower still, amidst ever-widening chasms, tossed and whirled about by waterspouts, and so ill lit by the red star of the lamp beneath him that the great moving shadows took on the shapes of streets and crossroads in some far away, devastated city."[9]

A series of passages from various works and authors will illustrate in detail how this static, spatially fixed perception of the city, with its well-defined standpoints from above, from street level and from below, determined the structure of the city image well into the nineteenth century; the last two examples, from Hugo's *Notre Dame* and Dickens' *Our Mutual Friend*, will show how this static view was beginning to destabilize, and the word-city was starting to move.

Although Paris was a figure in literature long before the nineteenth century, Balzac was chiefly responsible for transforming it into a myth.[10] The extraordinary passion with which he fused realistic description, literary rhetoric, and his own intense love-hate ambivalence toward the city and all it stood for set the model of "Paris" for French literature as far ahead as Proust.

Balzac's choice of spatial standpoints was always shrewd. In depicting urban life he usually preferred the horizontal street-level view. But he understood the uses of elevated perspective and employed it to dramatic effect, as in the symbolic contrasts between Angoulême, on its rock, and L'Houmeau below it in *Lost Illusions*. At the close of *Père Goriot*, Eugène de Rastignac stands above Paris in the cemetery of Père Lachaise, where Goriot has just been buried. Rastignac surveys the city of the living from the vantage point of the city of the dead, which doubles Paris and underscores the many ambivalent attitudes conveyed in this short scene:

"Rastignac, left alone, took several steps toward the top of the cemetery and saw Paris lying tortuously along the two banks of the Seine, where lights were beginning to shine. His eyes attached themselves almost greedily between the column of the Place Vendôme and the dome of the Invalides, there where that high society lived into which he had wanted to penetrate. Toward this humming hive he threw a glance which seemed to suck out its honey in advance, and uttered these grandiose words:

" 'Now it's between the two of us!'

"And as his first act of defiance against society, Rastignac went to dine with Mme. de Nucingen."[11]

At this concluding moment Balzac wants to elevate his own and his character's perspective above the horizontal melodrama which has been the substance of *Père Goriot*. From the height of the cemetery the living city is presented in two interesting metaphors. The first, that of the city "lying tortuously along the two banks of the Seine" is a personification, with the person-city prone in a position of suffering or great discomfort. There is a paradox in "tortuously lying," a contradictory yoking together of tension and repose. This contrasts with the second image, which is one of abundance and purposeful energy: the humming beehive, of which (ambivalence in another form!) Rastignac sees himself as the future despoiler.

One of Balzac's well-recognized characteristics is to subordinate his characters, never to allow them to fill completely the stage on which they act. The vision is not theirs but the author's; he alone achieves the real elevation in this scene. Rastignac fails to rise to the empty challenge he sets himself, as he has failed to rise to real ones throughout the novel. He also fails to fill the imposing setting Balzac has placed him in; he remains a small character looking down on the city of life from the elevated city of death. Instead of the philosophical soliloquy which the funeral of Goriot and the setting would seem to demand, Rastignac can only utter a challenge which the author editorially calls "grandiose." When we meet Rastignac again later in Balzac's comedy, in *Lost Illusions*, he has become a cynical and calculating member of the social establishment he had so despised and desired in *Père Goriot*.

Closer examination of this scene reveals that it actually contains three cities: the physical city of Paris, the intangible city of high society within it, and the city of the dead, both tangible and intangible, in which Rastignac has been placed by his author. These three conflicting cities overshadow the unheroic character who is belittled by his author. Rastignac rejects the panoramic sweep of the physical city to single out the small area marked by two fixed monuments as the domain of high society, *le monde*. This small world itself is not visible; it consists of people's lineage, money, and attitudes, and its values are arbitrarily determined abstractions. His focus on this small city excludes the larger one. Rastignac, looking down from the cemetery, can only see the spatial markers defining the unseen boundaries of fashion. Even this spatial center is represented by a grammatical void: Rastignac's eyes "attached themselves . . . between" (*s'attachèrent . . . entre*) the two monuments. They do not attach themselves *to* anything. In looking down at the city, Rastignac finally focuses on emptiness.

One of Hawthorne's short parables shows in exemplary fashion how a writer uses an elevated vantage point to describe a city fixed in space. "Sights From a Steeple" appeared in *Twice-Told Tales* in 1837. With Hawthorne's typical lucid complexity it describes what a first-person narrator "sees" from the top of an urban steeple. This story has the clarity of thought about it rather than the clarity of observation (Poe called it an essay); the speaker, a stand-in for the poet or writer, seems to be describing a projected image rather than an actual scene. The speaker's gaze proceeds from the sky to the horizon to the country to the ocean and finally to the town below him: "In three parts of the visible circle, whose center is this spire, I discern cultivated fields, villages, white country seats, and the waving line of rivulets, little placid lakes. . . . On the fourth side is the sea, stretching away towards a viewless boundary, blue and calm, except where the passing anger of a shadow flits across its surface, and is gone. . . . On the verge of the harbor . . . is a town; and over it am I, a watchman, all-heeding and unheeded."[12]

The "town" the speaker describes is actually a port city, bustling with commercial activity and containing its appropriate residential and business quarters. Hawthorne uses the smaller word "town" for specific effect. It is a more intimate term than "city," and shrinks the spatial perspective, like looking at something large through the wrong end of a telescope. This diminishing is a deliberate sign, corresponding to the placing of the city within the larger spatial framework of sky, country, and ocean. The word "town" also allows the elevated spying poet to establish a greater intimacy with the various human dramas he sees below him: Several young people and an old man provide the unseen seer with material for a deduced drama; a funeral, after colliding with a parade of soldiers, arrives at the graveyard at the foot of the poet's steeple; and finally a thunderstorm, which gradually builds up and breaks upon the scene, drives the poet from his coign of vantage, but not before he has a final glimpse of the rainbow.

Fatality hovers over all these inventions. The small drama of young love meets with parental objection and is brushed aside; the busy world of the port brings to the poet's mind the complementary vision of ships and cargo strewn over the bottom of the sea; the soldiers look like toys; the funeral reminds the poet of historical attitudes toward death; the coming of the rain and the breaking of the storm, which scatter all the human figures, are seen as an apocalypse; and, startlingly, the city of the living now appears to the observer like a city of the dead. But his final glance at the apparent judgment of the heavens on sea, country, and city is lightened by signs of clearing in the west and the appearance of the rainbow.

The spatial elements in "Sights From a Steeple" are all fixed in relation to each other, and are presented allegorically. If they were more elaborated, Hawthorne would have his reader looking at Homer's shield of Achilles; if, on the other hand, the slight movements of clouds and people (a function of the observer's distance from them) were frozen, this parable would present the teasing landscape of Keats' Grecian urn.

Within this near-fixity the poet's imagination is the force which moves, up, down, out, even as far as things not to be seen from the steeple, the interiors of houses. The narrating voice is disembodied, the elevated voice of poetic imagination. (In a similar essay, Hugo von Hofmannsthal called the poet "the soundless brother of all things."[13]) Higher than man, lower than God, the poet's eye has the unique power to look both up and down, to see things, as we say, in perspective. But the poet's elevated position dooms him to look at civilization from the detachment which distance entails, in spite of his longing to see life up close. "O that the Limping Devil of Lesage would perch beside me here, extend his wand over this contiguity of roofs, uncover every chamber, and make me familiar with their inhabitants!" Hawthorne's speaker exclaims. "The most desirable mode of existence might be that of a spiritualized Paul Pry, hovering invisible around man and woman, witnessing their deeds, searching into their hearts, borrowing brightness from their felicity, and shade from their sorrow, and retaining no emotion peculiar to himself."

The city in "Sights From a Steeple" is the place where man's life, affairs, and death intersect within the larger harmonious circle of nature. The city is seen from above by the artist, whose encompassing view links the transient and visible with invisible archetypes. Underlying the bustle of seen or imagined city life are the pattern and mystery of things.

In *The Spleen of Paris*, Baudelaire adopted a much less charitable stance above the teeming city:

My heart content, I climbed the mountain
From which one can contemplate the city in all its breadth,
Hospital, brothel, purgatory, hell, prison,

Where every monstrosity blossoms like a flower.[14]

Whether he was describing an observed scene at all—the details in these lines are abstract, the tone ironic, the "breadth" of the city is narrow—remains, as so frequently with Baudelaire, an open question. In any event Baudelaire, like his beloved cats, loved high places from which he could contemplate the restless activity of the horizontal city whose streets he knew so well.

The poem called "Landscape" was first published in 1857, under the title "Parisian Landscape." In the 1861 edition of *Flowers of Evil* Baudelaire placed this poem, revised and with its shortened title, as the first in a section called "Parisian Tableaux."[15] "Landscape" is thus the initial poem in a series whose specific theme is the big city. The others are street-level poems, but this overture looks at the city from above and sets in motion complicated currents of themes and feelings.

I want, in order chastely to compose my eclogues,
to lie near the sun, like the astrologers,
and, neighbor to the bell-towers, listen while dreaming
to their solemn hymns carried away by the wind.
My chin in my two hands, at the top of my garret,
I will see the workshop which sings and chatters;
the chimneys, the steeples, these masts of the city
and the vast skies which make one dream of eternity.

It is sweet, through the mists, to see born
the star in the blue, the lamp in the window,
the rivers of carbon climb to the firmament,
and the moon pour forth its pale enchantment.
I will see the springs, the summers, the autumns;
and when winter shall come with its monotonous snows
I will close everywhere doors and shutters
to build in the night my fairylike palaces.
Then I will dream of bluish horizons,
Of gardens, of fountains weeping in alabasters,
of kisses, of birds singing evening and morning,
And all those things most childish which the idyll contains.
Riot, tempesting in vain my windowpane,
will not cause me to raise my head from my writing-desk;
for I shall be plunged into this voluptuousness
of evoking spring with my will,
of drawing a sun from my heart, and of creating
out of my burning thoughts a mild atmosphere.[16]

To call a city poem "Landscape" was undoubtedly startling
at the time, and sets up an immediate discord. The "tableaux"
of the general title are pictorial in both a theatrical and a moral
sense, which derive from the late eighteenth-century concepts
of Diderot and Mercier, whereas "landscape" is a more specific term borrowed from painting, of which Baudelaire was
an astute critic. Both "tableaux" and "landscape" refer to
static settings.

In what ways can this poem be considered a landscape? Baudelaire seems to be transferring the poetic scene from country to city. More specifically, the poem presents a "painted" cityscape which is the equivalent of a landscape painting. The poem also contains a dream countryscape and refers to two pastoral forms of lyric poetry, eclogue and idyll. Unlike the other poems in this section of *Flowers of Evil*, these visions are not far removed from hallucination, and there is a suspicion that this poem might have been written under the influence of hashish. But even if this were the case, the tight organization of words and ideas in "Landscape," as well as our knowledge of Baudelaire's work habits, show a deliberate process of intellectual integration at work. In the last four lines of the poem, finally, a landscape is the image for the work of art which the urban poet creates out of his inner self.

In the *Salon of 1859* Baudelaire had written that "if such and such a collection of trees, of mountains, of waters, and of houses, which we call a landscape, is beautiful, it is so not through itself but through me, by my own favor, by the idea or feeling I attach to it. It is enough to say, I think, that any landscapist who does not know how to translate a feeling through an assemblage of vegetable or mineral matter is not an artist." These things need "an intelligence which can bring them to life."[17]

Thus the center of this poem can be located not in the scenes it describes or evokes, but in the mind which does the describing and evoking. "Landscape" also raises the interesting question of whether the poet is actually looking at a real scene, or of whether his garret—indeed the whole poem—exists only in his mind. The poem is one of intention ("I want," "I will") rather than realization. It might even be that the city imagery in the poem was inspired by an artist's rendering of the city. In the *Salon of 1859* Baudelaire has this reaction to the engravings of Meryon:

"I have rarely seen represented with more poetry the natural solemnity of an immense city. The majesties of accumulated stone, the belfries pointing their fingers to the sky, the obelisks of industry vomiting toward the firmament their combinations of smoke, the prodigious scaffoldings around monuments under repair, applying to the solid body of the architecture their temporary architecture of such paradoxical beauty, the stormy sky, charged with anger and bitterness, the depth of the perspectives, increased by the thought of all the dramas they contain: None of the complex elements of which the sorrowful and glorious decor of civilization is composed was forgotten."[18]

This description anchors the floating visions of "Landscape," in which the speaker imagines himself looking out of a garret window in the fixed position of a gargoyle above the city ("my chin in my two hands"). What is free to move in the poem is the poet's imagination, which can transform what it "looks" at—the "sorrowful and glorious decor of civilization"—or plunge inward away from the actual scene (if anything is real in this exquisitely subjunctive poem). The poet, physically above the city, is both contemplator and visionary. He imagines himself looking down on the industrial city and turning it into poetry. He sees chimneys and steeples as masts of a ship, smoke as rivers of carbon; he blots out the city by imagining himself looking up at "the vast skies which make one dream of eternity." His projected glance becomes double and he sees (or imagines) the blue and the lamp in the window. The moon pours forth its pale enchantment in vain on the smoky and commercial city.

In the seasonal and explicitly visionary part of the poem the city is—or will be—excluded from "direct" view. It will be outside the concrete reality of doors, shutters, and windowpanes. The city will be the source of riot, but safely below the poet. The ultimate vision of which the poem speaks is produced from within the poet and does not contain the city at all.

However, as the self-conscious language of this poem shows, the poet is not able to lose himself completely in his vision. He speaks of it as future while he remains in the present. This "time block" might account for the impression the poem gives that the poet is burdened by a heavy weight which drains his visions of energy and keeps him from realizing them. He lives, after all, in the modern industrial city; the distance from it to the never-never land of a rhetorical romanticism is simply too great for him to encompass except as an ambivalence he cannot resolve. The gargoyle's fixed position of contemplation above the city serves as a point of departure for the poet's floating mind as it tries to flee from the inescapable reality of the city.

In the poems which follow "Landscape," the poet descends to the horizontal labyrinth of the street and the daily lives of city people, including himself. All these poems begin with the fixed relationship of streets and people; the second poem has the sun striking and transforming both as the poet stumbles "over words as over paving-stones." The titles of some of the other poems indicate their spatial orientation: "To a Red-Haired Beggar Woman"; "The Seven Old Men"; "The Little Old Women." The series ends with "Dawn," a remarkable urban poem which hangs effortlessly between naturalism and allegory.

Common to all the poems in "Parisian Tableaux" is the exclusion of the poet from daily life. He is as removed from the city when he prowls the streets as he is imagining himself above the city in his garret. The contrast is even sharper when he comes down into the streets: The contemplator enters the world of action but cannot join it. His city is a paved solitude.

The city is also a paved solitude, but in another sense, for Emma Bovary. On one of the Thursdays when she is riding in the "Hirondelle" to Rouen for an assignation with Léon, Flaubert has the coach pause above the city:

"Sloping down like an amphitheatre, and drowned in the

fog, it overflowed unevenly beyond its bridges. Then the open country mounted again in a monotonous sweep until it touched in the distance the elusive line of the pale sky. Seen thus from above, the whole landscape seemed frozen, like a picture; the anchored ships were massed in one corner, the river curved round the foot of the green hills, and the oblong islands looked like giant fishes lying motionless on the water. The factory chimneys belched forth immense plumes of brown smoke, their tips carried off in the wind. One heard the rumbling of the foundries, mingled with the clear chimes of the churches, dimly outlined in the fog. . . . From time to time a gust of wind would drive the clouds towards the slopes of Saint Catherine, like aerial waves breaking silently against a cliff.

"Something seemed to emanate from this mass of human lives that left her dizzy; her heart swelled as though the hundred and twenty thousand souls palpitating there had all at once wafted to her the passions with which her imagination had endowed them. Her love grew in the presence of this vastness, and filled with the tumult of the vague murmuring which rose from below. She poured it out, onto the squares, the avenues, the streets; and the old Norman city spread out before her like some incredible capital, a Babylon into which she was about to enter."[19]

These disjointed successive paragraphs offer two different views of the same city. The first is controlled, "frozen, like a picture," although in this frozen picture little wisps of motion indicate, like the twitching of a cat's tail, a suppressed tension. The second drowns the city in the vague palpitations of Emma's feeling.

This vision of the city seems curiously bifocal in another way. In the first paragraph the narrator presents the city as an object in the reader's line of sight. In the second paragraph this visible city triggers and then disappears behind a non-specific vocabulary of passionate feeling. The city has become a screen on which this feeling is projected. The images of Emma's passion add a legendary and mythical resonance to the text which is beyond the capability of the pictorial description, tied as it is to the reality of the scene. Thus, under the flood of Emma's feeling, the Rouen of the present becomes historical ("the old Norman city") and beyond that Babylon, the capital city of a legendary sinful past. "Babylon" points the way forward again through time toward a consummation (in Léon's arms) in the near future. It is the expectation of this tryst which leads Emma to drown the city in anticipatory passion. In this sense her fog doubles the narrator's.

(Flaubert certainly knew where to find the jugular veins of his contemporary readers. The comparison of staid Rouen to sinful Babylon—is it the narrator's comparison or Emma's?— and the idea of the wanton Emma entering this Babylon in the hurtling "Hirondelle" to commit adultery "while the well-to-do residents of Bois Guillaume sedately descended the hill to town in their little family carriages" is one of the slashes of his finely-honed blade.)

Victor Hugo's tremendous popular success in his lifetime makes the cultural patterns evident in his prose and poetry especially interesting. Among the most important of these patterns is the image of the city, of which we have already seen one example from *Les Misérables*. Hugo's view of the city is historical and apocalyptic; his visualization of it is almost entirely architectonic in conception and architectural in interest. He might be called the Michelangelo of French literature: one pictures Hugo on a high scaffold at an immense distance, painting figures in a vast fresco, or, alternatively, sculpting rugged statues out of words. His created Paris is raised to the level of cosmic myth while at the same time retaining an acute rendering of realistic detail. (Baudelaire, though acknowledging his enormous debt to his older contemporary, disliked the cosmic part: "He moves in the immense without getting dizzy," he said of Hugo once.[20])

The combination of fixed spatialization and an acute sense of cultures shifting in time results in a curious tension in Hugo's picture of the city. His is a Paris of historical local color swirling around large monuments—Notre Dame, the Arch of Triumph, the Quarter of Thieves, even the sewers.[21] Hugo consciously attaches these monuments to the roots of the human psyche and civilization. The city is the crux of his myth-making. His urban characters, frequently half-allegorized or half-demonized, derive their force from the city, which looms over them in every sense.

The image of the city is central in *Notre Dame de Paris*—the title is the name of Paris' most famous monument. Although there is no lack of Parisian color in *Les Misérables*, the city there generally serves as a highly charged background. In the two novels the city is fixed in space, but doubled in time: Hugo places the action in the past while maintaining an obtrusively present narrative perspective, that of the time of writing. The full title of Hugo's cathedral novel, which was published in 1831, is *Notre Dame de Paris, 1482*. (*Les Misérables*, as previously stated, deals with events between 1815 and 1832 but was written between 1845 and 1862.) Thus the historical cities of the novels acquire a doppelgänger, the contemporary city, which is not exactly a shadowy presence in either work. Hugo does not preserve the appearance of historical verisimilitude (as Walter Pater does, for instance, in *Marius the Epicurean*), but in his capacity as authorial narrator shuttles back and forth in both novels between the past and the present. Here is a particularly direct example from *Les Misérables*:

> It is hard to imagine today what a country outing of students and shopgirls was like forty-five years ago. Paris no longer has the same environs; the image of what one might call circumparisian life has changed completely in this half-century. The cuckoo has given way to the railway coach; the barge has been replaced by the steamboat.

51

. . . The Paris of 1862 is a city which has all France for a suburb.[22]

Notre Dame de Paris overflows with architecture. Aside from the cathedral itself and an architectonic view of the Paris of 1482, the novel even includes a theory of urban architecture which makes Hugo read like a nineteenth-century Lewis Mumford. According to Hugo, architecture was man's first writing, his first fixing of cultural energy in a coherent, static form. In the Middle Ages the architecture and ornamentation of monuments, such as the cathedral, was the chief form of collective cultural expression at a society's command. Hugo, as a nineteenth-century writer looking "forward" in his novel from 1482, prophesies that the invention of printing will kill architecture as writing. Movable type will, as he puts its, obliterate the fixed letter of architecture, which until then had provided the "books" of civilization.[23]

In addition to this contrast between past and present, *Notre Dame* makes extensive use of our three levels of spatial viewpoint. Hugo uses a vertical scale to organize his highly charged picture of Paris. Human life goes on in the street; the upper regions belong to contemplative demons (Quasimodo and the gargoyles), the lower regions to mystery. At the very top of this vertical scale is the author himself, looking down on the city from above: A diurnal chapter entitled "A Bird's-eye View of Paris" in *Notre Dame* has its nocturnal counterpart, "An Owl's-eye View of Paris" in *Les Misérables*. In the earlier novel there is a constant shifting of standpoint from above to street level to below, with some complicated variations (Claude Frollo's subterranean alchemist's cell is actually located in the cathedral's tower; the dungeon of Esmeralda's mother is at street level).

Street level in *Notre Dame* is where the historical events of "1482" take place. It is the world of everyday life, a maelstrom of citizens, pageants, markets, pursuits, and assignations; it

contains all the local color of what might be called the Walter
Scott level of this novel. The cathedral soars above the life of
the street, and much of the novel's demonic action takes place
within it, mostly in the tower, above but in view of the street.
The cathedral also strikes down into the ground, so that it is
in fact the center of the church's body which is at street level.
Hugo pursues this thought in a remarkable passage:

"In the Middle Ages, when a building was finished, there
was almost as much of it in the ground as above. Unless it
had been built on piles, like Notre-Dame, a palace, a fortress,
a church always had a double foundation. In the cathedrals
it was, in a way, an other, subterranean cathedral, low, dark,
mysterious, blind and dumb, beneath the upper nave brim-
ming with light and resounding day and night with organs
and bells; sometimes it was a tomb. In the palaces and in the
fortresses it was a prison, sometimes also a tomb, and sometimes both together. These powerful buildings, whose manner of formation and of *vegetation* we have explained elsewhere, had not simply foundations, but, so to speak, roots
which ramified in the soil into chambers, galleries, and stair-
cases like the construction up above. Thus churches, palaces,
and fortresses had earth at mid-body. The cellars of a building
were another building, where one went down instead of up,
and which affixed its subterranean storeys under the stack of
the exterior storeys of the monument, like those forests and
mountains which reverse themselves in the mirroring water
of a lake beneath the bordering forests and mountains."[24]

Hugo is here not so much creating mythic significance as
identifying it. He is making explicit the implicit idea that the
city and its monuments express both man's intrusion on and
expiation of the mythic forces inherent in the natural world
(or, in modern terms, in the mind itself).[25] Hence the linking
of sky-surface-underground, cathedral-palace-fortress-prison-
tomb; the monument as artifact metaphorized in nature imagery; above all, the doubling of the visible world by another

which exists but is not ordinarily visible. Hugo's paragraph is a powerful statement of how the trees of civilization arise from underground roots, or, in less metaphoric terms, how the legends of storytelling arise from the myths of natural forces.

There is another passage in *Notre Dame* which is the apotheosis of Hugo's spatial way of presenting the city. This is Claude Frollo's vivid hallucination—actually a phantasmagoria—in which static elements of the urban scene, though keeping their fixity, are mixed into a picture of total confusion by changes in perspective. The towers of "up" and the Hell of "down" are mixed with the street level on which the unhappy churchman stands:

The sun had set behind the high Nesle Tower. It was the moment of twilight. The sky was white, the water of the river was white. Between these two whitenesses the left bank of the Seine, on which he had his eyes fixed, projected its dark mass and, diminished more and more by perspective, sank into the mists of the horizon like a black arrow. It was laden with houses, of which one could only make out the dark silhouette, vividly set off in darkness against the light background of sky and water. Here and there windows began to shine like holes of embers. This immense black obelisk, thus isolated between the two whitish sheets of sky and the river, which was quite broad at this point, had a strange effect on Dom Claude, comparable to that which a man would feel who, lying on his back at the foot of the bell-tower of the cathedral at Strasbourg, would see the enormous needle disappear above his head into the penumbra of the twilight. Except that here it was Claude who was standing and the obelisque which was lying down; but as the river, in reflecting the sky, prolonged the abyss beneath him, the huge promontory seemed as boldly launched into the void as any cathedral steeple, so that the impression was the same. This impression had in it something still stranger and more profound: It was indeed the Strasbourg bell-tower, but the Strasbourg bell-tower two leagues high, something unheard-of, monstrous, incommensurable, a building such as no human eye had ever seen, a Tower of Babel. The chimneys of the houses, the pinnacles of the walls, the shaped gables of the roofs, the spire of the Augustine, the Nesle Tower, all those sallies which breached the profile of the colossal obelisk added to the illusion in bizarrely figuring to the eye the cutouts of an intricate and fantastic sculpture. In his state of hallucination Claude thought he saw, saw with his very eyes, the belfry of Hell. The thousand lights scattered over the entire height of the frightful tower seemed to him like so many portals of the huge furnace inside; the voices and noises which issued from it so many cries, so many death-rattles. He was afraid, he put his hands over his ears in order to hear no more, turned his back in order to see no more, and ran away from the frightful vision. But the vision was within him.[26]

Frollo's phantasmagoria is a disturbance of visual perspective. Its elements are presented as static, and are carefully enumerated at the beginning in their normal relationship to each other (sun, tower, sky, river, and riverbank). The disturbance is indicated by the kaleidoscoping and magnifying of these fixed elements; it seems to be imposed on Frollo from the outside rather than emanating from his chaotic inner turbulence, even though the vision is said to be "within him." The description is architectonic; one sees a Hieronymus Bosch painting rather than a mind in turmoil. Frollo, of course, is the villain in a melodrama and not a study in psychology. Psychology of character was not something in which Hugo was greatly interested; he indicates inner complexity in characters in passing, but his main interest in them (as in the city) is in typification rather than individuation, in their possibilities as dramatic and even visual counters. The way in which Dostoevsky was to locate Raskolnikov's turbulence entirely within the mind of the character was not for Hugo. This is probably why his novels have been relatively neglected, for although they link up nicely with the popular novel of the later nineteenth and early twentieth centuries, they do not follow the "high road" which the complex novel took, the internalization of the external world.

In 1837 Hugo published a volume of poems entitled *Interior Voices*. It contains a remarkable ode which is called "To the Arch of Triumph," but which is actually the poet's meditation on Paris.[27] This poem shows an apocalyptic sense of historical time overwhelming the city of the present fixed in space. It begins with a rumination on its ostensible subject, which was a curious subject for this poem. Napoleon had begun building the Arch of Triumph in 1806 as a monument to his troops, but it was not finished and dedicated (by Louis Philippe) until 1836; thus the poem, set in the present, was a response to a brand-new monument commemorating a recent historical event. It is an oblique response. Hugo begins by tying the new monument to time (although not, oddly enough, to the occasion it commemorates) as perceived by a poetic mind representing universal human consciousness: "Age crowns and ruin completes. / The edifice needs a past of which one dreams, / Grief, triumph, or remorse." This is, of course, a past the new monument does not have, but, even without it, a monument is an expression of civilization. The absence of past is, indeed, at the center of the poem; the new monument will acquire one as the future of the city becomes another present. Civilization is the city; as in ancient cities, its center is the center of the universe: "Paris is the solemn place / Where the ephemeral eddy / Turns on an eternal center."

This long poem crystallizes Hugo's conception of the city

56

as a monument of monuments, but shadowed by the inexorable march of history toward its inevitable destruction. The city in the poem is an emblem of profound ambivalence for a poet whose thought seems to express a deep collective attitude towards culture. Paris is "somber fire or pure star"; "Brother of Memphises and of Romes / It builds in our century / A Babel for all mankind / A Pantheon for all the gods!" In running through the catalog of these glorious and legendary cities of the past, Hugo asserts that the new arch will be immortal because it is pure, whereas cities are built on spilt blood. There is a strong undertone here of guilt and of the destruction of the city as a form of expiation.

"To the Arch of Triumph" ends with the destruction of Paris. The poet has an apocalyptic vision of the city submerged beneath the flood. An elevated observer seated on a hill—the poet's own projection of himself in the future—sees the site of the city as a "supreme tomb": "An arch, a column, and over there, in the midst / Of the silvered flood whose foam one hears, / A half-wrecked church in the fog!" The surviving monuments are identified by their forms rather than their proper names; they have joined, in this vision, the ruins of anonymous monuments marking the heart of a dead civilization.

(This pattern of monuments being drowned by a flood recalls that several centuries earlier Rabelais had caused Gargantua, resting on the towers of Notre Dame, to repay the pestering hospitality of the citizens of the French capital by urinating on them "so fiercely that he drowned two hundred and sixty thousand, four hundred and eighteen persons, not counting the women and small children." This destructive inundation was also an act of baptism, since it led to the renaming of the city, formerly Lutèce—or "Leucetia," as Rabelais has it—Gargantua having acted only *par ris*, in sport.[28]

Like Hugo's Paris, Dickens' London is a powerful organizing image, which knits together the kinetic forces of character and action in his novels. Dickens' city is more pervasive in his fiction than Hugo's is in his, and less grandly architectonic; in atmosphere it is perhaps more like Baudelaire's Paris, an unstable nervous energy. Surely the cityscape of nineteenth-century literature would be unthinkable without Dickens' London, by turns real and surreal, grim, quirky, and always fascinating. In his earlier novels it is represented as a relatively coherent, fixed place; in the later ones it becomes a destabilized place bursting at the seams with barely controlled energy.[29]

It is this straining energy which makes Dickens' use of the convention of fixed narrative perspective in his later novels so interesting. Especially in his last completed novel, *Our Mutual Friend*, written in 1864 and 1865, Dickens presents the spectacle of a writer whose perception of the urban world as fragmented and unstable was ahead of the literary conventions and techniques, based on fixed forms and stereotypes, which were his stock-in-trade for presenting it.

The physical city in this final novel is everywhere surrealized; the seamy river-edge and the river itself, with heavy emphasis on death by water; the central importance to the plot of the city's refuse, those gigantic garbage mounds containing real and mythical fortunes; the former country houses (the Porters inn and Boffin's Bower) which have long since been swallowed up by the encroaching city; the new spreading urban blight, pushed outwards into the countryside by a burgeoning economy. With great virtuosity Dickens peoples this rich scene with representatives of a complex society which is off-center and under great strain: the urban poor, the upward strivers, the rootless nouveaux riches, the impoverished working class, the idle professionals, the criminals and police. The city, the locus of civilization, is the central brooding image in *Our Mutual Friend*. It is an agglomeration of crazed parts, of static elements whose relationship to each other has been jumbled and whose forms are incoherent. This creates a slight feeling of anxiety in the reader, who does not quite know what to expect next from the shifting recombinations of apparently familiar things and recognizable people. (One begins to see why Dickens was one of Kafka's favorite writers, and why *Our Mutual Friend* made such a strong impression on T. S. Eliot.)

As the result of this kind of tension the perspectives of urban space in *Our Mutual Friend*, while still apparently rooted in a static matrix, abound in fuzzy boundaries and sudden shifts. The unpredictability of these changes signals the weakening of the static representation of the city: The depths of the Thames give up bodies to the surface; a crazed old inn vibrates with life; a rooftop becomes a street-level setting in the sky and the outward push of the expanding city an aggressive act.

Dickens opens his novel by combining two of the most powerful archetypes in our culture, the city and the river. The river yields up the dead for purposes of capitalistic commerce—a combination of myth and money not unlike that in Wagner's *Ring of the Nibelungs*, composed about the same time Dickens was writing *Our Mutual Friend.*

How conscious Dickens was of this association of motifs can be seen in the novel's first sentence, in which he added the mythic past of primitive materials to the river flowing through the city: a boat "floated on the Thames, between Southwark Bridge which is of iron, and London Bridge which is of stone. . . ." The tide is running, and the boat seems to have risen to the surface from the depths: "Allied to the bottom of the river rather than the surface, by reason of the slime and ooze with which it was covered, and its sodden state, this boat. . . ." The still unnamed boatman too partakes of this peculiar juxtaposition: "Half savage as the man showed, . . . with such dress as he wore seeming to be made out of the mud that begrimed his boat, . . ."[30]

The reader learns that the man and his daughter earn their

living by fishing up and robbing corpses from the river. Thus the linked themes of death and profit are introduced. Shortly after, they are taken up by the main plot, which concerns the monetary gain resulting from the supposed drowning in the river of the heir John Harmon. Between this death and Hexam's robbing the corpses of the drowned, death and commerce are doubly allied as they rise into the modern city from the primal river. It was, of course, the river's normal trade which made the rise of London possible; Dickens adds the mythic as well as the social substratum to the city's power.

The association of city and river is significantly extended later in the novel in some important scenes set in the country, along the upstream Thames. This country, however, is not an idyllic opposition to the city, but is rather an extension of it along the river of industry, trade—and death. Betty Higden and Lizzie Hexam flee to towns up the river, seeking refuge and employment. The mortal struggle between Riderhood and Headstone takes place in a lock in the river in which both drown. Eugene Wrayburn is nearly killed on its banks. All the "country" scenes in this novel lead inexorably, like the canalized river itself with its locks, back to Dickens' London.

This city is not, like Hugo's, one of cultural monuments and picturesque crowds; it is characterized for the most part by eccentric people in bizarre dwellings, interspersed with descriptions of the urban scene which border on the surrealistic. One of the most striking buildings in *Our Mutual Friend* is the Six Jolly Fellowship Porters Inn. It is fixed in space, and presented as such, but everything about its fixity seems about to collapse and resolve the structure into its primordial elements:

"The Six Jolly Fellowship Porters, already mentioned as a tavern of dropsical appearance, had long settled down into a state of hale infirmity. In its whole constitution it had not a straight floor, and hardly a straight line; but it had outlasted, and clearly would yet outlast, many a better-trimmed building, many a sprucer public-house. Externally, it was a narrow lopsided wooden jumble of corpulent windows heaped one upon another as you might heap as many toppling oranges, with a crazy wooden verandah impending over the water; indeed the whole house, inclusive of the complaining flag-staff on the roof, impended over the water, but seemed to have got into the condition of a faint-hearted diver who has paused so long on the brink that he will never go in at all.

"This description applies to the river-frontage of the Six Jolly Fellowship Porters. The back of the establishement, though the chief entrance was there, so contracted that it merely represented in its connection with the front, the handle of a flat iron set upright on its broadest end. This handle stood at the bottom of a wilderness of court and alley: which wilderness pressed so hard and close upon the Six Jolly Fellowship Porters as to leave the hostelry not an inch of ground beyond its door.

"The wood forming the chimney-pieces, beams, partitions, floors and doors, of the Six Jolly Fellowship Porters, seemed in its old age fraught with confused memories of its youth. In many places it had become gnarled and riven, according to the manner of old trees; knots started out of it; and here and there it seemed to twist itself into some likeness of boughs. In this state of second childhood, it had an air of being in its own way garrulous about its early life. Not without reason was it often asserted by the regular frequenters of the Porters, that when the light shone full upon the grain of certain panels, and particularly upon an old corner cupboard of walnut-wood in the bar, you might trace little forests there, and tiny trees like the parent tree, in full umbrageous leaf."[31]

This public house is lopsided and decrepit, yet it does not collapse, but perversely exhibits a continuing vitality which seems to emanate from its primordial wood. Expressing as it does these two contradictory states, the inn is an exact reflection of the lopsided, decrepit, and yet still vital urban society it sits in the the midst of, which also exists in a state of "hale infirmity." The tension of this oxymoron is felt throughout the urban world of *Our Mutual Friend*.

The street-level picture Dickens paints of the Six Jolly Fellowship Porters is exactly parallel to his presentation of the urban scene in this novel: the surface is lopsided and eccentric, as at the Veneerings' parties, and the vitality is hidden and ambivalent. This hidden force expresses itself most strongly as negative power, as in Riderhood, the river, and Fascination Fledgeby; less strongly as an assertion of strength toward the end by the "good" forces, until then powerless or neutralized. In his description of the public house Dickens is also raising a contrast between present and past, and between surface and depth. The building apparently stood before it was engulfed by the wilderness of the city; it rises into the present out of its roots in the past. These roots, or more accurately the primitive dynamic wood of which the building is made, also strike the note of depth; the wood is presented as in some way a "racial" memory, if one may use this phrase of inanimate, but animated, matter. The tavern's function also brings a past which was closer to nature into the city: "Just as the pub is the center of village life, it creates the equivalent of the village—a neighborhood feeling—in the city."[32] In many ways, this image represents the survival into a decrepit present of earlier, deeper, more primitive instincts. The inn appears to be on the point of toppling into the fateful river; inn and river, throughout the novel, are associated with the most primitive of its characters, the savage Riderhood.

One scene in particular in this novel so disorients a fixed spatial standpoint that it might almost be taken as an example of flux. Its basic angle of view is elevated, but by comparison with the fixed viewing position of Hawthorne's high standpoint in "Sights From a Steeple" Dickens scrambles the three levels (sky, roof, street) of his scene. On the roof of the house belonging to the usurer Fascination Fledgeby, Lizzie Hexam and her crippled friend, Jenny Wren, have set up a quiet retreat, thus transposing ground level to the rooftop. Fledgeby has forced his way up to this retreat and cannot understand what the two girls, both powerless victims of the city, are doing there with his patient employee, Old Riah.

'We are thankful to come here for rest, sir,' said Jenny. 'You see, you don't know what the rest of this place is to us; does he, Lizzie? It's the quiet, and the air.'

'The quiet!' repeated Fledgeby, with a contemptuous turn of his head towards the City's roar. 'And the air!' with a 'Poof!' at the smoke.

'Ah!' said Jenny. 'But it's so high. And you see the golden arrows pointing at the mountains in the sky from which the wind comes, and you feel as if you were dead.'

The little creature looked above her, holding up her slight transparent hand.

'How do you feel when you are dead?' asked Fledgeby, much perplexed.

'Oh, so tranquil!' cried the little creature smiling. 'Oh so peaceful and so thankful! And you hear the people who are alive, crying, and working, and calling to one another down in the close dark streets, and you seem to pity them so! And such a chain has fallen from you, and such a strange good sorrowful happiness comes upon you!'

Her eyes fell on the old man, who, with his hands folded, quietly looked on.

'Why it was only just now,' said the little creature, pointing at him, 'that I fancied I saw him come out of his grave! He toiled out at that low door so bent and worn, and then he took his breath and stood upright, and looked all around him at the sky, and the wind blew upon him, and his life down in the dark was over!—Till he was called back to life,' she added, looking round at

Fledgeby with that lower look of sharpness. 'Why did you call him back?'

'He was long enough coming, anyhow,' grumbled Fledgeby.

'But *you* are not dead, you know,' said Jenny Wren. 'Get down to life!'

Mr Fledgeby seemed to think it a rather good suggestion, and with a nod turned round. As Riah followed him to attend him down the stairs, the little creature called out to the Jew in a silvery tone, 'Don't be long gone. Come back, and be dead!' And still as they went down they heard the sweet little voice, more and more faintly, half calling and half singing, 'Come back and be dead, Come back and be dead!'

. . .

Thus, Fascination Fledgeby went his way, and the old man went his different way up-stairs. As he mounted, the call or song began to sound in his ears again, and, looking above, he saw the face of the little creature looking down out of a Glory of her long bright radiant hair, and musically repeating to him, like a vision:

'Come up and be dead! Come up and be dead!'[33]

The "narrow," "close dark" streets of the everyday city, seen from above, become a kind of underground. The rooftop, as a kind of elevated street, enjoys the quiet and the air which the streets below lack. It is also presented as a downward extension of the sky. Dickens' turns of perspective in this scene play on the reader's cultural-mythic sense of death, the idea that when one dies, one's body goes below ground and the soul goes up to heaven. When Riah comes out on the roof from that "low door," so reminiscent of Blake's engraving, it is as if his resurrection is indeed happening; he is emerging from the "underground" of bodily death (equated with life in the empirical city below) to heaven. Thus when Jenny,

effectively surrounded by a halo, chants to Riah to "come up
and be dead," her paradoxical command or incantation is not
the contradiction it appears to be; she is summoning him to
the higher death of eternal life. Fledgeby is rejected for this
honor ("Get down to life!"). Since Fledgeby's life, unlike
Riah's, is without redeeming moral value, Jenny judges him
as not fit for the visionary company.

On a purely physical level, then, this episode is built around
a vertical urban scale of street, rooftop, and sky. But the
curious effect of the scene depends on the displacement between this descriptive physical level and the emblematic scale
of the moral drama in which Jenny appears as an angel from
above, Fledgeby as a quasi-devil from below (the level on
which the unconsidered life equals death, also an old idea in
Western culture), and Riah, although a Jew, is the soul who
is redeemed in this Christian minidrama, ascending from underground into the sky.

A different kind of urban vista in *Our Mutual Friend* involves
the aggressive expansion of the urban edge into the surrounding countryside. Dickens had a sharp eye for the details of
this process. As opposed to the static country town in, for
instance, Hardy's *Mayor of Casterbridge*, which has a sharp,
fixed boundary, Dickens' word-city oozes into the suburban
countryside:

> The schools . . . were down . . . where Kent and Surrey
> meet, and where the railways still bestride the market-
> gardens that will soon die under them. The schools were
> newly built, . . . in a neighborhood which looked like a
> toy neighborhood taken in blocks out of a box by a child
> of particularly incoherent mind, and set up anyhow; here,
> one side of a new street; there, a large solitary public-
> house, facing nowhere; here, another unfinished street
> already in ruins; there, a church; here, an immense new
> warehouse; there, a dilapidated old country villa; then,

a medley of black ditch, sparkling cucumber-frame, rank field, richly cultivated kitchen-garden, brick viaduct, arch-spanned canal, and disorder of frowziness and fog. As if the child had given the table a kick, and gone to sleep.[34]

The rhetorical surrealism of Dickens' language is here applied to a numbingly ordinary scene. In spite of such localizing naming as "where Kent and Surrey meet," the impression is strong that Dickens was not looking at a single scene but summing up the kaleidoscopic impressions of many. He gives the reader, as it were, the essence of urban edge; the passage is actually plural, but presents itself in the singular.

The schools as a figure in *Our Mutual Friend* are the domain of Bradley Headstone and Charley Hexam. Master and pupil are also new and raw, as is the society whose sudden jumbled expansion has made their rise possible. The new dynamism of society has enabled both Headstone and Hexam to leave the fixed order of their class to live in a landscape which is incoherent both socially and mentally. The school represents for both the mechanism of class escape into the new jumble of rootlessness. Thus this description of an incoherent scene is a subtle reinforcement of character. In analogous ways, Dickens uses other aspects of the city to characterize the root-edness of the Boffins and the rootlessness of Wegg, the Veneerings, Wrayburn, and the Laemmles.

Dickens is still bound, in this late work, to the conventions of the realistic novel. Yet the city in *Our Mutual Friend* is half in and half out of these conventions. Its buildings are still fixed to their spots, but at the same time they are both demonized and etherealized. Dickens' late word-city is well on the way to losing its moorings in the real world entirely, like the barracks in Georg Trakl's poem, which "flee through the afternoon" as a function of the speaker's melancholy.

The apotheosis of the urban edge was to occur some seventy

years after Dickens, in Rilke's *Tenth Duino Elegy*. In this poem the tawdry naturalistic landscape of the city and its edge are forced into allegory:

> Though, alas, how strange are the streets of the Pain
>   City,
> where in the false stillness, made of deafening din,
> strong, the casting from the mold of emptiness
> swaggers: the gilded noise, the bursting monument.
>   .   .   .
>
> But on the outskirts the edges of Fair are always curling.
> Swings of freedom! Divers and jugglers of zeal!
> And the figurative shooting-gallery of prettied-up
>   happiness,
> where the target wriggles and behaves tinnily
> whenever one more skilled hits the mark. From applause
>   to chance
> he tumbles on, for booths woo, drum, and bawl for
>   every curiosity.
>   .   .   .
>
> Oh, but just beyond this,
> behind the last plank, pasted with ads for "Deathless,"
> that bitter beer which seems sweet to its drinkers
> if they always chew fresh distractions with it . . .
> just in back of the plank, right in back, it's real.
> Children play, and lovers hold one another—apart,
> serious, in the sparse grass, and dogs act in nature.[35]

Rilke's Pain City stands for modern life. It is presented as totally false, a negative value. What is genuine and positive tentatively begins on the edge of this city, as the newly dead move out from the city of life into a stark landscape of early death toward the distant mountains of primal sorrow. The time journey in the conclusion of this elegy is represented as a space journey.

We have all seen ragged edges of cities; but who has really

looked at them or thought to make meaning out of them—in Rilke's case the climax of a philosophical meditation? Both he and Dickens saw the metaphoric possibilities in these images. Both moved them—to borrow Hofmannsthal's terms—from latent "pre-existence" in the mind of the reader (who has seen the phenomenon but not seen any significance in it) to "existence" (in which, by connection and association, the phenomenon is charged with meaning).

Rilke's Pain City is more abstract than Dickens' London, but both convey a strikingly negative attitude toward the city. Although the modern city is more than ever the locus of civilization, it is seen as a distraction from and a threat to a life of genuine meaning. City lives are empty or threatened; the victimization of city people by incoherent forces beyond their control seems unstoppable. Not that either writer is biased toward country life, which both see as containing its own terrors (Rilke in *The Notebooks of Malte Laurids Brigge*, Dickens in *Great Expectations*). In Dickens, especially in the late novels *Little Dorrit* and *Our Mutual Friend*, the city is a somber, brooding presence. It seems that Dickens' city people can be saved only by the sentimental conventions of Victorian fiction or, as many readers of *Our Mutual Friend* have noticed, by Dickens' recourse to the fairy tale. There is an ambivalence in this novel between the negative forces embodied in the presentation of the city and the desire on the part of Dickens and the literary convention of his day to end the novel tidily and prettily, so that the good characters can live happily ever after. Evocation of the magic world of the fairy tale, in the "lost prince" Harmon, the Cinderella-like "princess" Bella, the villainous Riderhood, the suddenly "good" and "bad" Boffins, and the sudden denouement, allows Dickens to resolve the problem. By appealing to the unreal reality of the fairy tale, a reality characterized by anxiety can be made acceptable.

At bottom, the city in *Our Mutual Friend* seems close to Freud's peculiar "eternal city" in *Civilization and Its Discontents*. Dickens seems to posit a primal world of instinctive forces still very much alive in the skewed modern city: raw aggression, sex, greed, the drive for dominance and power, and the sheer instinct for survival. As Dickens presents it, the modern city has failed to socialize these primal instincts. It is unable to accommodate the lives of decent people like Riah, the victim of the usurer Fledgeby, or Jenny Wren, a cripple with an alcoholic father, or Lizzie Hexam, who bears the triple cross of coming from the lowest class of society and having a criminal father and an upstart brother. The city's basic civilizing function in this novel is not strong enough to drive away the underlying primitive forces; it can only keep them in check, and not very effectively or consistently. The energetic characters in *Our Mutual Friend* are the primitives: Wegg, Riderhood, Headstone, and the "pretending" Boffin. They contrast strikingly with the pervasive ennui of Eugene Wrayburn and the helplessness of the others. The Porters Inn contains within its wooden structure its primal energy, the original forest from which it was built, but finds itself now located in the midst of the urban "wilderness."

Thus in Dickens' last completed novel human emotions are primitive and violent (Headstone, Riderhood) in spite of an overlay of social manners (Wrayburn, the Laemmles) and the presence of the conventionally genteel emotions of Victorian fiction (Bella and John, Mrs. Boffin, the "real" Mr. Boffin). Modern urban society is itself an institution without content (the Veneerings, Podsnap, Lady Tippins); the world of urban work is surrealistic (Young Blight looking at the graveyard from his office, Sloppy and Betty Higden, Jenny as the dolls' dressmaker, Mr. Wilfer and the counting-house). At the heart of *Our Mutual Friend* a strong primitive id seems to be struggling with a devitalized cultural ego. The figure of the city is emblematic, as in Freud's Rome, rather than symbolic, and seems most closely associated with the primitive forces. The city world in this novel is constantly threatening to turn Freud's metaphoric ideal on its head, and to announce that where ego is, id shall be—again.

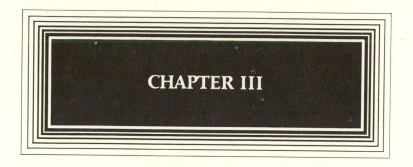

CHAPTER III

The City in Flux

Poe—It is most peculiar for one to find his vision of
the world in such fixed things, since in life everything
glides and flows.

—HOFMANNSTHAL

During the nineteenth century the word-city was increasingly
represented in literature as an unstable refraction of an individual consciousness rather than as an object fixed in space.
This change is part of a larger process, the increasing internalization of the external world, which was going on generally
in literature, music, much of painting, and psychology.[1] at
the same time a large part of European civilization, and the
part which dominated public attention, was going in the opposite direction: the explosion of empirical knowledge and
the mechanical wonders of the industrial revolution occupied
the center of the public stage, and the developing natural and
social sciences became increasingly concerned with the quan-
tification and classification of external characteristics. This
split, and the conflicts it produced, is of course one of the
great themes of nineteenth-century literature, as in Flaubert's
opposing pairs of characters, Emma and Homais, Frédéric
and Jacques Arnoux.

The city as a major literary topos reflected these opposing

attitudes. The difference between the empirical city (which remained as physically real as ever) and the subjectively perceived image of the city became increasingly marked.

The writer of the later nineteenth century no longer represented the city as a static space whose monumental parts stood in fixed relationship to each other, as in Madame Vauquer's monumental boardinghouse in *Père Goriot* or Hugo's cathedral. The word-city was presented more and more as an irritable nervous energy, and its inhabitants came to seem more prowlers than citizens. The new model was Baudelaire's changeable poet, for whom the city streets are shifting refractions of his moods. The idea that the city represented a stable community over a long period also faded; the instability of the outer world as seen by a solipsistic character or narrator reflected an increasing disorientation of the time sense as well as the space sense. Something of this was seen in the passages from Dickens, Freud, and Musil quoted earlier. Henry James mentions that one can develop associations with the staircase of a family house, but hardly with an elevator in a high-rise;[2] anonymity was replacing sociability, and quick money speculation was replacing values of long duration.

Since writers form their image of the city in response to the magnetic field of their culture, they are sensitive to changes in cultural attitudes. The figure of the city as a paved solitude took hold quickly. Even where characters were presented as part of a social group, they were increasingly shown in isolation from each other, and the groups themselves were seen as isolated from the larger social community. This is true of families (the Micawbers, the Marmeladovs, the Raskolnikovs) as well as of individuals (Micawber, Marmeladov, Mrs. Marmeladov, Raskolnikov, Prufrock). As a result of this changed orientation the city in literature became fragmented and transparent rather than tangible and coherent, a place consisting of bits, pieces, and shifting moods; it came to stand under the sign of discontinuity and dissociation rather than community.

The cities of Joyce, Woolf, Musil, Kafka, Eliot ("unreal city"), Howells, and Dos Passos represent the breaking of roots and the snapping of stems in terms of the coherence of urban life.

Since Baudelaire is an important exemplar of this change in sensibility as it involves the city, a consideration of his other aspect seems in order. In "Landscape" we saw the poet and the city imagistically fixed in their physical relation to each other while the poet's imagination roamed among other conceptions of space and time. In "The Swan" (1859) the poet is described in the shifting stance of moving at street level through a physically changing city, whose changes sound the insistent note of instability and exile in the poem.

The elements of this poem are presented as the response of the poet's mind to external urban stimuli; all these elements are in fitful motion relative to each other. The city in the poem is framework, sign, and catalyst. These various functions are expressed through, and intermingled with, images of the poet's memory, perception, and mood. The memory image spreads outwards from a past legend and a recent urban scene; the perception is the roaming poet's, of the physical city being torn down and rebuilt; the mood is one of dissociation and longing.

I.

Andromache, I think of you! This little stream,
Poor and sad mirror where once shone
The immense majesty of your widow's griefs,
This false Simois which grows by your tears

Has suddenly impregnated my fertile memory
As I was crossing the new Caroussel.
The Paris of old is no more (the form of a city
Changes more quickly, alas, than a mortal's heart);

I see only in my mind all this camp of barracks,
These piles of rough-hewn capitals and of shafts,

These weeds, the large blocks greened by the water of
    puddles,
And, shining on the paving stones, the confused bric-a-
    brac.

There in other times a menagerie was spread out;
There I saw one morning, at the hour when beneath
    skies
Cold and clear Work awakens, where road-making
Pushes a dismal hurricane into the silent air,

A swan which had escaped from its cage,
And, with his webbed feet scraping the dry pavement,
Dragged his white plumage over the rough ground.
Near a waterless gutter the beast, opening his beak,

Nervously bathed his wings in the dust,
And said, his heart filled with his beautiful natal lake:
"Water, when will you rain? When will you thunder,
    lightning?"
I see this unhappy creature, strange and fatal myth,

Sometimes stretching its avid head on its convulsive neck
Toward the sky, like the man in Ovid,
Toward the ironic and cruelly blue sky
As if it were addressing reproaches to God!

II

Paris changes! But nothing in my melancholy
Has budged! New palaces, scaffoldings, blocks,
Old neighborhoods, everything becomes allegory for me,
And my cherished memories are heavier than rocks.

Thus before this Louvre an image oppresses me:
I think of my great swan, with its mad gestures,
Like exiles, ridiculous and sublime,
And gnawed by a desire without relief! And then of you,

74

Andromache, fallen from the arms of a mighty husband,
Abject chattel, under the hand of proud Pyrrhus,
Bent in rapture near an empty tomb;
Widow of Hector, alas! and wife of Helenus!

I think of the emaciated and consumptive negress,
Stamping in the mud and seeking, with haggard eye,
The absent coconuts of superb Africa
Behind the immense wall of fog;

Of whoever has lost what is not to be found again,
Never, never! Of those who are steeped in tears
And who suckle Grief like a good she-wolf!
Of gaunt orphans withering like flowers!

Thus in the forest where my mind exiles itself
An old Memory blows the bugle with full force!
I think of the sailors forgotten on an island,
Of captives, of the conquered . . . of still many others![3]

In "The Swan" thoughts of exile crystallize in the poet's mind around the idea of the city. Through the litany of exile one hears the underlying antiphony: places of belonging, places of banishment. The city is always one of these poles, but not always the same one. Andromache, Victor Hugo (to whom the poem is dedicated), and the poet's mind are exiled *from* cities. The swan and the negress are exiled *to* the city. The poet is also exiled *in* the city. The old city itself, now destroyed, has been driven into exile in the poet's memory to be replaced by the new, unfinished one, whose physical fragments surround him. Toward the end of the poem the poet's vision expands to include a universe of exiles; one feels that if he had not stopped himself in time his catalog would have gone on to include everything. Yet this expansion is at the same time a contraction, the poet's withdrawal from the outside world into his own existential isolation.

"The Swan" telescopes heterogeneous fragments. Literary

motifs and echoes from Vergil and Ovid mingle with anthropological and sociological insights and the rhetoric of Romanticism, against an unspoken background of politics. The poet's mind projects this jumble of elements onto the city, which is presented as an emblem of unstable motion and discontinuity. The radical disjunction between the deconstruction of the old city and the construction of a new one makes the city figurally transparent, a sign rather than an object. (The title already contains this ambiguity, since in French "cygne," swan, and "signe," sign, are homonyms.)

The changing city is connected with the poem's strong pathos. Exile is a geographical concept, a loss of an original place in which one naturally belongs. The displacement of exile banishes this belonging to the memory, and creates the idea of dissociation from the new home. The expulsion from Eden is the archetype of exile; as Proust says, the only true paradises are the paradises one has lost.[4] In "The Swan," the swan has lost its "beautiful natal lake," the negress has lost "superb Africa," and the poet has lost his city. The new Paris is a different city of the same name in the same place, perhaps the cruelest form of exile for the poet who continues to inhabit it.[5]

In two other notable poems, Baudelaire presents the city under the sign of flux. In them it is not exile which is the sign of dissociation, but the city's change in state from night to day and day to night. In "Dawn" (*Le Crépuscule du matin*, 1852; another edition gives 1843), and "Twilight" (*Le Crépuscule du soir*, 1852), the poet presents night and day as separate, self-contained worlds discontinuous with each other. Night is the time for crime, frenzy, savagery, demons, debauchery, death, sleep, and dreams. Day is the time for the shuffling drudgery of the world of work. The moment of both poems is the transition from one state to the other. Proust and Kafka were later to be fascinated by moments of waking up and going to sleep, but they were to root these moments in a

76

character's conscious or semi-conscious mind. Baudelaire roots them in the city. It is the city and not the poet which is waking up and "waking down." In both poems the city is seen in the flux of transition. As the debauchees of night return home at dawn, "broken by their labors" (*brisés par leurs travaux*), Paris emerges as an allegorized figure, "le sombre Paris," an old workman rubbing his eyes at the break of day and reaching for his tools.

Both poems bear witness to the increasing assimilation of literature to modern urban rhythms of space and time—fragmented, short-range, immediate. Work and pleasure are alike reduced to a dull routine of alternating habits. The city has obliterated the countryman's clear and simple division of day and night; the internal organization of the city around its own day and its own night in "Dawn" and "Twilight" has blotted out the awareness of any other order of things. Compared with the Romantic poetry of the preceding generation, Baudelaire's has redefined nature as urban. It is a small step from Baudelaire's Paris to the fragmented cities of Eliot, Joyce, Rilke, and Brecht.

In Whitman's poem "Crossing Brooklyn Ferry,"[6] everything is in motion. The poet is standing on the ferry as it crosses the East River between Manhattan and Brooklyn; the locus of the poem is his consciousness. The multitude of passengers on the ferry who excite the poet's imagination are on their way home to one city from work in the other. Whitman had been a newspaper reporter and a compulsive pounder of the streets of New York and Brooklyn; both people and port were a constant delight to him, and he had always had, he tells us in *Specimen Days*, "a passion for ferries; to me they afford inimitable, streaming, never-failing, living poems."[7] A sharpness of observation in "Crossing Brooklyn Ferry" attests to Whitman's canny eye for urban reality, and yet the poem presents this reality in largely generalized terms. This was deliberate on Whitman's part; he wanted to raise the images of himself as poet, the two cities, their working population, and the water-crossing to universal and mystical significance.

"Crossing Brooklyn Ferry" is a poem of the self; its center of gravity lies in the vision of the poet rather than in the objects enumerated, which are made transparent by the overwhelming power of his vision. The city of monuments and buildings is conspicuously absent; what Whitman gives us are other attributes of the city: the crowds of workers and their stations in life, the port with its ships, transportation, and trade, and not least himself as denizen of the city.

The peculiar stage of this poem is the empty space between two cities. This space is a river, which is at the same time both the East River in New York and simply *a* river. As in *Our Mutual Friend*, the mythic archetypes of city and river are combined with commerce. The ferry is the essential link and necessary bond of communication between the two cities; it is also a bond between the poet and mankind, and between past, present, and future. On the one hand the poem's images suggest the timeless mythic level of an archetypal pattern, such as the souls of the dead being ferried across the Styx (Whitman's crowded ferry anticipates the crowds flowing across the river over London Bridge in Eliot's *The Waste Land*); on the other hand this poem is emphatically historical, a vision of past and future proclaimed by a poet speaking in the present tense.

Everything in "Crossing Brooklyn Ferry" is in motion relative to everything else: water, tides, history, people, even the pronouns.[8] The poet himself, at the center of both archetypal and historical worlds, is moving with the crowd relative to the offstage cities. His marginal perception of them changes as the relative position of the moving boat changes. He also looks down at the water and up at the sky. Relativism is basic to this world, which tries to include everything in human life and to establish a unifying pattern among its elements:

78

> The simple, compact, well-join'd scheme, myself
>   disintegrated, everyone disintegrated yet part of
>   the scheme,
> The similitudes of the past and those of the future,
> The glories strung like beads on my smallest sights and
>   hearings, on the walk in the street and the passage
>   over the river,
> The current rushing so swiftly and swimming with me
>   far away,
> The others that are to follow me, the ties between me
>   and them,
> The certainty of others, the life, love, sight, hearing
>   of others.

The city of the future becomes the place in which the unique personal identity of the speaker will be a voice from the past— a living presence repeated in the individual people of the future:

> . . . distance avails not, and place avails not,
> I too lived, Brooklyn of ample hills was mine,
> I too walk'd the streets of Manhattan island, and bathed
>   in the waters around it,
> I too felt the curious abrupt questionings stir within me.
> In the day among crowds of people sometimes they came
>   upon me,
> In my walks home late at night or as I lay in my bed
>   they came upon me,
> I too had been struck from the float forever held in
>   solution,
> I too had receiv'd identity by my body, . . .

The beginning of the poem takes us from the "flood-tide below me" and the "clouds of the west" to "crowds of men and women . . . on the ferry-boats . . . returning home." In the third section of the poem Whitman sketches a natural world of water and birds, the busy port, and the fires of foundries on shore at night. However, this whole section of apparent observation is set back in the past. All the verbs are in the past tense ("watched," "saw," "look'd"); it is not night (the sun in the west is "half an hour high"). The poet also makes clear that he is referring not to just one but a long series of crossings—"I too many and many a time cross'd the river of old"—suggesting both his earlier life and earlier incarnations.

This third section of the poem, which is apparently the most specifically descriptive, turns out on closer examination to be a generalized summation of many experiences telescoped into the description of one experience. But this description is not generalized to the point of erasing its particularity: the time of day is given, crowds are going home from work, the poet presents a harbor which can only be New York harbor. It could not be mistaken for Boston or Philadelphia, even apart from its identification in the title and text of the poem; Whitman's port is too large, the rhythms of its activity and people too hurried, even the rhythm of the poetry itself too expansive for it to be any other place. In its sense of place "Crossing Brooklyn Ferry" is far more specific than the London of Wordsworth's "Westminster Bridge."

The final section of "Crossing Brooklyn Ferry" is an intensified reprise of the individual elements of the poem. A series of invocative imperatives admonish natural and mechanical processes to go on doing what they are already doing in the harbor of the great city.

The burden of Whitman's poem is not the urban area itself but its positive transillumination. The pedal points of the poem are the elements of air, earth, water, and fire; the four points of the compass; the past, present, and future, and the poet himself as an individual consciousness transcending his historical life span. The East River is not, in fact, very wide, but Whitman manages to make a short ferry trip into a mythic voyage. The narrow space between the cities is expanded from reality to idea; it is transcendentalized, but as the result of energy imposed by the poet's will rather than energy which flows to the poet from a reality he is observing. He imposes his vision, he does not deduce it. The deliberateness of this vatic stance can be underlined by placing beside it a realistic description from an American novel of the same period. The usually rarefied Henry James describes an urban scene in *The Bostonians* like this:

> [One could see] a few chimneys and steeples, straight, sordid tubes of factories and engine shops. . . . There was something inexorable in the poverty of the scene, shameful in the meanness of its details, which gave a collective impression of boards and tins and frozen earth, sheds and rotting piles, railway-lines striding flat across a thoroughfare of puddles . . ., loose fences, vacant lots, mounds of refuse, yards bestrewn with iron pipes, telegraph poles and bare wooden backs of places.[9]

In spite of the narrator's editorial comment, this scene is presented as it might appear in reality. It is not energized, transcended, or transcendentalized into a higher vision. (It would take a Rilke, in the *Tenth Duino Elegy*, to do that with a similar description.) By contrast, one begins to see how insistent is Whitman's drive to rise through the physical sordidness of industrializing America. Practically speaking, of course, even the intensity of Whitman's vision could not transcend this particular reality for longer than the space of a poem, and his utopian visionary city would later be debased into the alabaster chimera of "America the Beautiful."

Whitman was as aware as James of the reality behind the vision. In *Democratic Vistas* there are some eloquent pages in which he conjures up the visionary potential of the real America and then shatters his own vision on the rock of actuality. This minisermon is worth quoting at length, because

81

it indicates the extent to which the city is central to Whitman's thought as well as his conscious awareness of empirical reality. After roundly condemning the social values, politics, religion, and literature of his day, he continues:

After an absence, I am now again (September 1870) in New York City and Brooklyn, on a few weeks' vacation. The splendor, picturesqueness, and oceanic amplitude and rush of these great cities, the unsurpassed situation, rivers and bay, sparkling sea-tides, costly and lofty new buildings, façades of marble and iron, of original grandeur and elegance of design, with the masses of gay color, the preponderance of white and blue, the flags flying, the endless ships, the tumultuous streets, Broadway, the heavy, low, musical roar, hardly ever intermitted, even at night; the jobbers' houses, the rich shops, the wharves, the great Central Park, and the Brooklyn Park of hills (as I wander among them this beautiful fall weather, musing, watching, absorbing)—the assemblages of the citizens in their groups, conversations, trades, evening amusements, or along the by-quarters—these, I say, and the like of these, completely satisfy my senses of power, fullness, motion, etc., and give me, through such senses and appetites, and through my aesthetic conscience, a continued exaltation and absolute fulfillment. Always and more and more, as I cross the East and North rivers, the ferries, or with the pilots in their pilot-houses, or pass an hour in Wall Street, or the Gold Exchange, I realize (if we must admit such partialisms) that not Nature alone is great in her fields of freedom and the open air, in her storms, the shows of night and day, the mountains, forests, sea—but in the artificial, the work of man too is equally great—in this profusion of teeming humanity—in these ingenuities, streets, goods, houses, ships—these hurrying, feverish, electric crowds of men, their complicated business genius (not least among the geniuses), and all this mighty, many-threaded wealth and industry concentrated here.

But sternly discarding, shutting our eyes to the glow and grandeur of the general superficial effect, coming down to what is of the only real importance, Personalities, and examining minutely, we question, we ask, Are there, indeed, *men* here worthy the name? Are there athletes? Are there perfect women, to match the generous material luxuriance? Is there a pervading atmosphere of beautiful manners? Are there crops of fine youths, and majestic old persons? Are there arts worthy freedom and a rich people? Is there a great moral and religious civilization—the only justification of a great material one? Confess that to severe eyes, using the moral microscope upon humanity, a sort of dry and flat Sahara appears, these cities, crowded with petty grotesques, malformations, phantoms, playing meaningless antics. Confess that everywhere, in shop, street, church, theatre, barroom, official chair, are pervading flippancy and vulgarity, low cunning, infidelity—everywhere the youth puny, impudent, foppish, prematurely ripe—everywhere an abnormal libidinousness, unhealthy forms, male, female, painted, padded, dyed, chignoned, muddy complexions, bad blood, the capacity for good motherhood decreasing or deceased, shallow notions of beauty, with a range of manners, or rather lack of manners (considering the advantages enjoyed) probably the meanest to be seen in the world.[10]

This poem in prose, with its homeric cataloguing series, also generalizes particulars. It does so, however, not in the celebratory form of "Crossing Brooklyn Ferry," but rather in the castigating manner of a sermon, rhetorically decrying the physical and ethical deficiencies of urban society as it is. The problem, as Whitman sees it, is that the complexities of the modern city are a magnificent human achievement and contain resources created by positive human energies, but the inhabitants of "these cities" show all the signs of degeneration rather than the regeneration their environment should call forth. Even to the vatic imagination ambivalence is the sign of the city. Instead of resolving this ambivalence, Whitman goes on in *Democratic Vistas* to call for a new literature.

Thus the willed upbeat vision of "Crossing Brooklyn Ferry," written before and revised after *Democratic Vistas*, derives not from naive faith on the poet's part, but from his awareness that the reality he wishes for is the opposite of the reality he sees; the former is only potentially present in the latter. His poem is exhortatory, designed to raise what he would call in his prose sermon the "flippancy and vulgarity, low cunnning, infidelity" of the people by sheer mental force (his own) to the level of the ideal.

But this imposition of a transforming will on the rawness of the physical world produces a peculiar sense of strain in "Crossing Brooklyn Ferry." The central space in the poem, the harbor, is a hollow space. The cities and their business and social activity surround it, but like an empty shell seen from the inside. The ferry itself is a shuttle between the two shores, but across nothingness. The poem rests on three dimensions, horizontal, vertical, and temporal, which do not intersect except in the mind of the traveling poet. Standing on the deck of the ferryboat he looks up at the sky and down at the water as well as at the horizontal hustle of port, people, and cities. This enables him to introduce a vertical dimension of timeless contemplation into the horizontal everyday world. He imposes a large, transcending spacetime on a smaller and limited one. The dimensions intersect in his Self, which expands greatly in the course of the poem from the individual to a kind of World-Self, leading to the final exhortations:

Thrive, cities—bring your freight, bring your
    shows, ample and sufficient rivers,
Expand, being than which none else is perhaps more
    spiritual,
Keep your places, objects than which none else is more
    lasting.

"Being" seems here to refer to consciousness, "objects" to
the bits and pieces of physical reality, such as the ferryboat,
which are the counters of consciousness. "Cities," in this
obscure triad, seems to serve as the larger organizing principle
representing the ingathering of human endeavor, bringing it
to a point of concentration one might call the critical mass for
the imagination of the poet.

    But—to believe *Democratic Vistas*—real cities were not thriv-
ing in the ethical sense; if one believes "Crossing Brooklyn
Ferry" itself, objects were not keeping their places, but were
in constant, relativistic motion. On the other hand, the poet's
being was certainly expanding, at least in an exhortatory
sense, bent on transformation of a refractory urban world.
This view of the city is highly solipsistic; Whitman's experience of the ferry crossing and crossings, the multitude of his
fellow-passengers, the cities, and the visions which grow out
of these elements, are private. He is not expressing values he
shares with his beloved fellow-citizens, but values he wants
them to have. The poet in "Crossing Brooklyn Ferry" is the
lonely sermonizer, like Hölderlin's Empedocles or Nietzsche's
Zarathustra. The city represents the major problem which
must be overcome, the estrangement of the growing urban
population from cultural values and culturally based ethics—
the difference between *Gesellschaft* and *Gemeinschaft*, in Tönnies'
famous formulation, which also dates from Whitman's time.
    Hart Crane, who included a direct homage to Whitman in
his epic poem *The Bridge* (1930), picks up this intense act of

will bent towards a future better than the present. As Crane apostrophizes Whitman:

> O Saunterer on free ways still ahead!
> Not this our empire yet, but labyrinth
> Wherein your eyes, like the Great Navigator's without
>   ship,
> Gleam from the great stones of each prison crypt
> Of canyoned traffic. . . .[11]

In rejecting the city's physical reality in favor of an inner vision, Whitman was doing in his own way what many of the writers of his time and later did, retreating from the external city to an internal one. He transcendentalized it as Baudelaire had allegorized it and Proust was to memorialize it. By the end of the nineteenth century the literary convention of the city had become for most a paved solitude. As for the Brooklyn ferry, it soon became a crossing in the mind: Brooklyn Bridge was opened to traffic on May 24, 1883, to become in its turn a new myth, Hart Crane's "intrinsic Myth . . . / Forever Deity's glittering pledge," the organizing urban emblem of Crane's epic poem about America.

In James Thomson's poem "The City of Dreadful Night" (1870-74), the city is a private emblem of quite another kind than Whitman's or Crane's. This city bodies forth an inner angst and black melancholy, only slightly turned to the outside.[12] Thomson, a kind of English Poe, led a dim and alcoholic life; this was the only one of his poems which struck a spark with a wider public. It is an extreme manifestation of the pessimism found in Matthew Arnold and Hardy and in the combination of aesthetic luxury and angst in the London of *The Picture of Dorian Gray* and the various adventures of Sherlock Holmes.

Thomson's long poem is interesting because of the way in which he uses the static city as an organizing metaphor for his mental anguish. The imagined, unreal, and unnamed metropolis in "The City of Dreadful Night" is a city-state of melancholy, a limbo for those who, like the narrator, are neither alive nor dead, and totally without hope. One of the epigraphs of the poem is the first line of the inscription above the gate of Hell in Canto III of Dante's *Inferno*: "Per me se va ne la città dolente." This quotation takes the reader back to the Christian vision of the city of Hell, but for Thomson this city is devoid of value, an empty container which projects his solitude:

> A river girds the city west and south,
>   The main north channel of a broad lagoon,
> Regurging with the salt tides from the mouth;
>   Waste marshes shine and glister to the moon
> For Leagues, then moorlands black, then stony ridges;
> Great piers and causeways, many noble bridges,
>   Connect the town and islet suburbs strewn.
>
>   . . .
>
> The city is not ruinous, although
>   Great ruins of an unremembered past,
> With others of a few short years ago
>   More sad, are found within its precincts vast.
> The street-lamps always burn; but scarce a casement
> In house or palace front from roof to basement
>   Doth glow or gleam athwart the murk air cast.
>
> The street-lamps burn amidst the baleful glooms,
>   Amidst the soundless solitudes immense
> Of rangèd mansions dark and still as tombs.
>   The silence which benumbs or strains the sense
> Fulfils with awe the soul's despair unweeping:
> Myriads of habitants are ever sleeping,
>   Or dead, or fled from nameless pestilence!
>
> Yet as in some necropolis you find
>   Perchance one mourner to a thousand dead,

So there; worn faces that look deaf and blind,
  Like tragic masks of stone. With weary tread,
Each wrapt in his own doom, they wander, wander,
Or sit foredone and desolately ponder
  Through sleepless house with heavy drooping head.

This fixed, hallucinatory city is a reification of the poet's feelings. It is imaginary, unlike Dürer's "Melancholia" and the Sphinx, referents in the empirical world which figure explicitly and at length at the end of the poem. Drawing and statue are conventional allegories of melancholy and inscrutability, but the most remarkable feature of this poem is Thomson's invention of a city as the reifying emblem of his desolation in the face of life. His sad and silent city looks forward to the urban deserts of de Chirico. Thomson's poem is an extreme example of how the image of the city was coming to stand for solitude rather than community; neither Heaven nor Hell, but Limbo.

Another important change in the literature of the nineteenth century is the gradual weakening of the topos of the country versus the city, which had been a convention of European literature since Vergil. As society became more urban and less rural, a disturbance of the values conventionally associated with this topos (the city as a place of wearying bustle, the country of pastoral harmony) began to appear in literature. Odd lapses of response to pastoral nature occur. In Baudelaire's "Landscape" the pastoral forms of eclogue and idyll are reduced to abstract names, but the city is, relatively speaking, vivid. In *Sentimental Education* (1869), Flaubert takes this warping of the stock response further. In one of the few rural scenes in this city novel, the hapless Frédéric and the courtesan Rosanette are driving aimlessly around the countryside while the Revolution of 1848 is going on in Paris. The narrator presents the landscape as a romantic pastoral idyll of great beauty; he even pauses to limn a painter painting.

Unlike the narrator, however, the two characters are worse than oblivious to this beauty, they are simply incapable of responding to it. Rosanette, who has grown up as an urban courtesan, may be forgiven this blankness; Frédéric, however, both grew up in the country and has exalted visions of himself as a great future poet, dramatist, novelist, and painter. Frédéric's defective sense of reality can only respond—and even that none too well—to the rapid succession of present, quick, discontinuous moments of life in the city, to impressions as distractions. Like the poet in "Landscape," Frédéric can only dream exotic idylls, but unlike the speaker in Baudelaire's poem, who hopes at least to create fairy-tale visions from within himself, Frédéric is totally a creature of velleity. In Flaubert's novel as in Baudelaire's poem, the city is the unique organizing matrix of the represented scene.

If London and Paris were the central mythic cities of European culture in the eighteenth and nineteenth centuries, the ambiguity of St. Petersburg in Russian literature offers an interesting view of the city from a position at the edge of this culture. Fate and history combined to give the capital of Imperial Russia a singularly vivid potential for mythification. In contrast to the long accretion of cultural capitals like London or Paris, St. Petersburg sprang like a latter-day Minerva from the head of Peter the Great. This remarkable monarch decreed the construction of this city on a marsh, out of nothing, in 1703. Called into being by the will of an emperor, architecturally patterned on Western rather than native models, intended as a window on the West for a backward and profoundly non-European culture, instant capital of a far-flung empire: small wonder that both the real St. Petersburg and the word-city of the same name stirred up ambivalent reactions in Russian culture.

"A newly founded city possesses a relatively simplified structure as against its parent model," a modern sociologist writes, "for its starting point is inevitably a simplified version of the terminal stage of a developed city."[13] This probably explains why the narrator of Dostoevsky's *Notes from Underground* calls Petersburg "the most abstract and intentional city in the whole world. (There are intentional and unintentional cities.)"[14] One might look at the cities of America's east coast the same way, but there is an important difference: although they were modeled on European cities ("terminal stage" is perhaps too strong), they and the new country were both founded at the same time, as part of the same culture. St. Petersburg, however, was a foreign body imposed on a long-standing culture of a quite different kind. It was, Philip Rahv writes,

> far more the capital of the Russian empire than of the Russian land. It was erected on the Finnish marshland with cruel haste and at the cost of many lives by the edict of Peter the Great, who undertook, with the savage rationality typical of belated and alien converts to progress, to transform his backward domain all at once into an efficient state militarized along modern lines. The self-will and precipitate style of this operation brought into being a city without roots in the past or in the vast rural hinterland, the center of alienation and of everything novel and foreign violating the national traditions and patriarchal mode of life.[15]

St. Petersburg was also protomythic in another way. As a water-city, built on a marsh and crisscrossed by canals leading into the Neva River, it is subject to frequent floods. The idea of the destruction of the city by flood (the conclusion of Hugo's poem "Arch of Triumph") is in this case a natural image. Indeed one critic, in tracing the myth of Petersburg from the founding of the city, notes that in its history "the periodically recurring inundations, the pressure of an angry sea on the daringly erected city, announced to the city by cannonades in the awful autumn nights, evoked images of the ancient myths. Chaos was seeking to swallow up the created world."[16]

The great flood of 1824 figures as the major event in Pushkin's haunting poem "The Bronze Horseman," written in 1833. Although in the preface to this poem Pushkin speaks lovingly of the city, the poem itself tells of a great disaster which befalls it—the flood—and the undeserved terrors which haunt and unhinge a blameless young hero who had been looking forward to a life of innocent happiness. On the way to see his fiancée he pays a ferryman for transporting him, but he finds that his fiancée's house has been swept away. He hallucinates that the bronze statue of Peter the Great, the founder of the city, comes to life and relentlessly pursues him through the streets of the city. The horror of this ambivalent poem suggests Poe and Hawthorne, as well as Kafka. In "The Bronze Horseman" the ambivalence is rooted in the image of the flooding of the city; retribution for unknown sins overtakes the innocent hero and the beloved city.

The flooding of the city is also connected with the most ambivalent character in Dostoevsky's *Crime and Punishment*, Svidrigaylov. This strange man hates water, even in paintings. On the night which ends with his suicide, he is drawn to the window of his cheap hotel by a violent storm. The city is flooding. The sound of the warning cannon shots produce in him a short, bitter vision:

" 'Ah, the signal! The water is rising,' he thought; 'towards morning, in the lower parts of the town, it will swirl through the streets and flood the basements and cellars, the sewer rats will come up to the surface, and amid the rain and the wind people will begin, dripping wet and cursing, to drag their rubbish to the upper floors. . . .' "[17] Svidrigaylov envisions the flooding of the city; his imaginings reveal this flooding as an image of his own mind, whose destructive libidinal impulses—he is intending suicide—threaten to rise as water and rats overwhelm his consciousness. This vision is immediately followed by a hallucination, Svidrigaylov's discovery in the "hotel corridor" (actually, of course, in his own mind) of the lecherous little girl. The next morning brings Svidrigaylov and the reader back to the real world: "A thick milky mist covered the city. Svidrigaylov walked along slippery, greasy, wooden pavements towards the Little Neva. His mind still held the illusory vision of its waters rising in flood during the night. . . ." Within the fictional text, Svidrigaylov walks through the "real" city, which is opposed to the hallucinatory image in his mind. It is in this "real" city that Svidrigaylov shoots himself. In *Crime and Punishment* Svidrigaylov functions as Raskolnikov's repressed libido; his suicide is an indispensable preparation for Raskolnikov's confession and eventual redemption. As Raskolnikov's crime had been an urban crime, defined in terms of the anonymity and depersonalization of this rootless city, Svidrigaylov's death is an expiation which destroys the city as a hallucination of the mind and restores it as a real, ordinary place without affect.

How does this depersonalized, morbid city square with Dostoevsky's ebullient newspaper pieces? A sometime journalist like Whitman, Dickens, and Baudelaire, Dostoevsky was an attentive stalker in, and of, the real St. Petersburg. In one of his *feuilleton* pieces he describes impressions of it this way:

> Here one cannot take a step without seeing, hearing, and feeling the contemporary moment and the idea of the present moment. It may be that in a certain regard everything here is caricature: but on the other hand, everything is life and movement. Petersburg is both the head and heart of Russia. We began by speaking about the architecture of the city. Even all this diversity testifies to a unity of thought and a unity of movement. This row of buildings of Dutch architecture recalls the time of Peter the Great. This building in the style of Rastrelli recalls

the century of Catherine; this one, in the Greek and Roman style, the latest time; but all together recalls the history of the European life of Petersburg and of all Russia. Even up to the present Petersburg is in dust and rubble; it is still being created, still becoming. Its future is still in an idea; but this idea belongs to Peter I; it is being embodied, growing and taking root with each day, not alone in the Petersburg marsh but in all Russia, all of which lives by Petersburg alone. . . ."[18]

The ebullience of this paragraph, embracing this city still in process, stands in contrast to the morbid shock registered by the poet in Baudelaire's "Swan" in response to the rebuilding of Paris. But Paris had been, until the mid-nineteenth century, largely a medieval city. What, in this young capital, did "Dutch architecture," the Western-oriented architect Rastrelli, or "Greek and Roman style" have to do with Russia? For the journalist Dostoevsky these foreign elements seem to bring in a breath of fresh Western cultural air. But the novelist Dostoevsky presents a more shadowed city. The association in this *feuilleton* of precise urban details and abstract ratiocination by the observer is also typical of *Crime and Punishment*. In this respect Raskolnikov's thinking parallels Dostoevsky's, except that the author has developed his character's and his city's schismatic natures in a negative direction. In the novel, the city without roots is the necessary scene of the rootless solipsist and his grandiose ideas of a more perfect moral order. It is only in this particular city that this particular kind of madness can thrive. "Nowhere else, in his opinion," writes Vyacheslav Ivanov of St. Petersburg and Dostoevsky, "did the *genius loci* produce so dreadful a fever of the soul. . . .

"Is not St. Petersburg itself . . . a purely imaginary and contrived conception?" Ivanov goes on to ask. "Is not its relation to the essence of Russia like that of a mirage to reality, of a deceitful mask to the true countenance? Is not the 'St.

Petersburg period' in Russian history the epoch of the great cleavage between actuality and appearance; of a form of consciousness—presumptuous and illusory, because its roots in the nation are snapped—which withers up man's sense of his organic union with Mother Earth, and thus of the living reality of God and of the world?"[19] (Ivanov's statement has even more point when applied to the apotheosis of the St. Petersburg novel, Biely's *St. Petersburg*.)

Two features of the image of the city in *Crime and Punishment* are especially striking: it is restricted to a limited topographical area, consisting mostly of one of St. Petersburg's seedier neighborhoods, and the naturalistic realism with which Dostoevsky describes this small part of the city makes it expand to fill almost the entire space of the novel. The streets, routes taken by the characters, and distances between points in the book are readily identifiable in the real world, so much so that a current edition informs the reader that "a map of St. Petersburg in Dostoevsky's time, showing locations important in *Crime and Punishment*, will be found on pp. 468-69."[20] Yet this is a word-city, and in spite of Dostoevsky's careful realism of detail it functions more as a projection of Raskolnikov's mind than as an independent setting within which Raskolnikov acts. Dostoevsky's novel concentrates almost exclusively on character and plot: although its fictive city is real enough to be mapped, it is nowhere in the narrative foreground, as it frequently is in Balzac and Dickens. The author's working notebooks for *Crime and Punishment* show the same emphasis.[21] Where, then, does the impression of the city's power in this novel come from?

A clue perhaps lies in Dostoevsky's statement that in St. Petersburg "one cannot take a step without seeing, hearing, and feeling the contemporary moment and the idea of the present moment." This suggests that in the novel the city operates as a series of sense stimuli, and that what these stimuli communicate is the rootlessness of a present without a past inherent in this city from its founding. Thus St. Petersburg forms and feeds the characters in *Crime and Punishment* without having to be spotlighted in the way Balzac's Paris and Dickens' London are. Dostoevsky's notebooks confirm what the novel indicates, that he, like Baudelaire, experienced the city as a total environment thoroughly internalized and assimilated in his personality and outlook. Dostoevsky transferred this trait to the characters of *Crime and Punishment*. Therefore, although he presents pictures of only a limited part of St. Petersburg, cityspace fills the entire novel from inside the characters as they move from room to room, flat to flat, through the streets, to the police station, and so on.

The city in this novel, then, is a necesssary and all-pervasive context for the action, but it is not itself in the foreground of the action; the reader's attention is focussed on the tensions and conflicts among the characters. The characters could not, however, function as they do anywhere but in this rootless, totally present, mythic, and alien capital city. Because the details of the literary city are made to correspond closely to the external topographical reality of St. Petersburg, they anchor the fantastic action of the story in an apparently familiar world.

How this works can be seen in a paragraph at the beginning of *Crime and Punishment*. The description of the locale is not a "set piece," first presented in narrative and then connected with the central character by having him enter the "scene"; rather, the disorder of the city corresponds to the disorder in Raskolnikov's mind:

> The heat in the streets was stifling. The stuffiness, the jostling crowds, the bricks and mortar, scaffolding and dust everywhere, and that peculiar summer stench so familiar to everyone who cannot get away from St. Pe-

tersburg into the country, all combined to aggravate the disturbance of the young man's nerves.

. . . An expression of deepest loathing passed across the young man's delicate features. . . . Soon, however, he relapsed again into profound thought, or rather into a sort of abstraction, and continued on his way in complete and wilful unconsciousness of his surroundings.[22]

Crime and Punishment is so thoroughly a city novel that it allows of no Rousseau-like contrast between urban corruption and country idyll. References such as the one above ("everyone who cannot get away from St. Petersburg into the country") are passing, and serve as a benchmark for the middle-class reader rather than imputing any value to the country. What we hear of the society of the provincial town where Raskolnikov, his mother and sister, Lhuzin, and Svidrigaylov come from makes it sound as demented as the Petersburg we see. Even the epilog begins: "Siberia. On the bank of a wide remote river stands a town, one of the administrative centres of Russia; in the town is a fortress, in the fortress is a prison." The only moment in the novel not claustrophobically urban is the final one, in which Raskolnikov, contemplating the vast open steppe (a desert rather than a pastoral landscape), envisages for the first time the possibility of a new life. But here the opposition is "closed-open" (city-town-fortress-prison/steppe), not "city-country."

In *St. Petersburg* (1910-11), Andrey Biely carries the emblematic city of Pushkin and Dostoevsky to an apocalyptic extreme. Biely's characters are much weaker than those in *Crime and Punishment*; indeed, they may be called recessive. This relative pallor of the characters serves to bring into prominence the real subject of the novel, the city. This city is both artificial and rootless in the present, and emblematic of a totally incoherent social order; even the social disorder in this novel is incoherent. The technique is prismatic: St. Petersburg is presented at various times impressionistically, expression-istically, pointillistically, realistically, and phantasmagori-cally. There is a narrative line in the novel, the "story" of the characters, but the sights, sounds, and colors of the city itself shift ceaselessly in and out of focus.

This Petersburg in flux contrasts with the scurry of its in-habitants in the revolutionary fervor of 1905; principally the stiff old bureaucrat Ableukhov and his son Nikolai, a latter-day version of Dostoevsky's underground man. The father has no flexibility, the son no fixity. Nikolai is neurotic, and a pathetically timid toyer with revolution. Out of weakness, he regrets having once offered to a terrorist group to blow up his father, and being taken up on it. They give him a bomb in a sardine tin, and both Nikolai and the reader wait through-out the novel for it to explode.

Biely starts to spin the web of his word-city in the prologue: "Petersburg is not merely imaginary; it can be located on maps—in the shape of concentric circles and a black dot in the middle; and this mathematical dot, which has no defined measurement, proclaims energetically that it exists; from this dot comes the impetuous surge of words which makes the pages of a book; and from this point circulars rapidly spread."[23] Later in the novel one character tells another: "Yes, this, *our* capital city, . . . belongs to the land of spirits—conventional references do not apply here. . . . Petersburg is a four-dimensional body, . . . and is only marked on the maps with a dot; this dot is where the surfaces of existence come into contact with the global surfaces and the tremendous as-tral cosmos."[24]

The empirical city in *St. Petersburg* is treated as a diaphanous idea which links present and past, East and West, and which also reflects the schizophrenia of pre-Revolutionary Russia caught between present and past, and East and West. Having established the transparency of St. Petersburg as his first prin-ciple, Biely "sees through" it in various ways. In describing

97

a sunset in colors of blood and fire, he transilluminates the city in a vision suggesting its fiery destruction:

> An enormous red sun hovered above the Neva; the buildings of Petersburg seemed to have dwindled away, transformed into ethereal, mist-permeated amethyst lace; the windows reflected the golden glow; the tall spires flashed rubies; and fiery flares invaded the recesses and the projections and set fire to the caryatids and the cornices of the brick balconies.
>
> The palace flamed blood-red; Rastrelli had built it: in those days the old palace had stood like an azure wall amid a series of white columns; the Empress Elizaveta Petrovna had gazed upon the stretches of the Neva. In Alexander I's day the palace had been repainted yellow; during Alexander II's reign, it was repainted again, this time a ruddy red.
>
> Slowly the rows of walls darkened against a waning lilac sky; sparkling torches burst into flame; and slight flames flared up here and there.
>
> The past was glowing in all this.[25]

The past glows in another way in *St. Petersburg*, in the repeated appearances of Pushkin's vengeful bronze horseman, the statue of Peter the Great. As in Pushkin's poem, here too the hero who founded the city becomes the vengeful instrument of its destruction. His role is that of a wrathful god. Biely seems to identify this malevolent statue as the *genius loci*, the reigning spirit of the city. Even on the mythic level, the sign of ambivalence hangs over an expiring society:

> The clouds were torn, and a green vapor was wafted from the seemingly melting bronze to drift in the moonlight, which suddenly flowed through the clouds. For an instant everything burst into light: the water, the roofs, the granite. The Horseman's face and his crown of bronze

laurels were ablaze, and so was that ponderous arm stretched out in an attitude of command. The arm seemed to shake, the rearing metallic hoofs seemed about to crash down on the rock, and the Horseman's voice seemed to resound through Petersburg:

'Yes, yes, yes . . . it is I . . . I destroy—irretrievably! . . .'[26]

Biely's vision of the city in this novel is impressionistically apocalyptic. It shows the flying apart under irresistible centrifugal forces of a city which since its founding had never been a coherent unifier of Russian culture.

After the Revolution of 1917, St. Petersburg was renamed Petrograd. As part of the demystification of Czarist Russia, the new rulers moved the capital of the country back to Moscow in March, 1918. (Moscow had not been the capital of Russia since 1712.) In 1924, after the death of Lenin, Petrograd was renamed Leningrad. In mythic terms, it was re-founded in the image of a new hero, but its two hundred years as a mythic emblem of the stresses of Russian culture were over. Lenin, the new hero, was buried in Moscow instead of in "Lenin City"—the ancient gesture of planting the dead hero-founder at the center of power.

CHAPTER IV

Individual and Mass

Two extreme types of actors show up with increasing fre-
quency in the fragmented word-city of nineteenth- and early
twentieth-century literature. The figure of the alienated and
isolated middle-class individual, frequently an artist, has its
roots in the literature of the late eighteenth century and the
Romantic period. A crowd of people as an undifferentiated
mass, acting as a depersonalized collective character and
forming a peculiar kind of anti-community within the dissociated culture, appears in literature some hundred years
later. In a few works these two types are directly opposed:
a withdrawn, sensitive, but devitalized individual confronts
a passionate mob which has power but no insight.

The gradual ascendancy of the dynamic, kaleidoscopic
model of the city, discussed in the preceding chapter, reflects
many displacements in the social structure of the Western
industrializing nations. Cities were places of witness to the
growing loss of shared conventions and values, with consequent weakening of the social fabric. In literature an interesting pattern developed, which associated this increasingly
fragmented view of the city with a radical reduction in the
power and grasp of the fictive hero. Aside from Baudelaire's
poet, there is a whole parade of small men in the novels of

the period who are unable to cope with their urban environment or with themselves, and whose attempts to cope lead to constant frustration. A partial list would include Flaubert's Frédéric Moreau, Dostoevsky's underground man and Raskolnikov, Hardy's obscure Jude, Joyce's Bloom, Kafka's two K.s, Howells' Silas Lapham, and Eliot's Prufrock, as well as Biely's Nikolai Ableukhov.

An interesting subset of these urban protagonists in nineteenth- and early twentieth-century literature consists of weak artists, who are intended by their authors to represent important attitudes about the possibility—or more likely the impossibility—of art in their time. These weak artists try with great difficulty and little immediate success (or occasionally too much) to rise to the high demands of Art. Their problems, however, are more bourgeois than aesthetic, as Thomas Mann's Lisabeta Ivanova shrewdly points out to Tonio Kröger. Among these weak artist figures are Balzac's Lucien Chardon and Wenceslas Steinbock, Rilke's Malte Laurids Brigge, the narrator in Proust's *In Search of Lost Time*, and Mann's Tonio Kröger and Gustav von Aschenbach. (Aschenbach's willed self-discipline carries him far but not far enough.)

These weak heroes and artists are intensely involved with cities. Their creators use the city thematically to represent the isolation or alienation of the individual within the culture. Joyce, Kafka, and Musil, for instance, present isolated individuals moving within cities which for most of the other characters are communities. The protagonists are excluded from these communities and feel their exclusion, although at the same time they may reject the communities as inferior or ignorant (Bloom and Stephen Dedalus against Dublin, Ulrich against Viennese society and politics). The basic tensions of *Ulysses*, *The Trial*, *The Castle*, and *The Man without Qualities* arise from this intra-urban exile.

There is a more radical disjunction in Rilke's *The Notebooks of Malte Laurids Brigge* and Eliot's *The Waste Land* and *Prufrock*. In these works it is not only the central character who is existentially isolated, but everyone. What few moments of community are shown are seen as accidental and transitory conjunctions. Walter Benjamin called Paris the capital of the nineteenth century; Rilke's Malte, a poor Danish poet, comes to this capital of European culture, but in the notebooks which he writes there Paris is seen not as the city of light but as the city of death and disease. The very first entry in *The Notebooks of Malte Laurids Brigge* starts off, after identifying the time as September and the place a street in Paris:

"Well, so people come here to live. I would rather believe this is the place of dying [*es stürbe sich hier*]. I have been out. I have seen: hospitals. I have seen a man who tottered and collapsed. People gathered around him, that spared me the rest. I have seen a pregnant woman. She pushed herself along with difficulty by a high, warm wall, which she groped for from time to time as if to convince herself whether it was still there. Yes, it was still there. Behind it? I searched on my map: Lying-in Hospital. Good. They will deliver her—they can do that."[1] Malte, the man who collapses, the pregnant woman, the "they" who will deliver her—all are radically separated from each other and from community in this Paris which consists on the one hand of the random and disconnected people and events which Malte "sees" (or records having seen), and on the other of the map of Paris, that abstraction which pretends to relate places to each other topographically in the real world. This first series of images of dissociation is repeated many times throughout this novel; the people in the reading room of the *Bibliothèque nationale*, each buried in his book and totally oblivious of the others; the row of patients waiting in the hospital, each, as Malte sees them, terrifyingly hermetic, yielding nothing to the observer beyond their surface appearance.

Malte is blocked rather than devitalized. This young poet

is unable to organize his impressions into a coherent aesthetic structure, but his individual impressions are, in themselves, intellectually coherent and extremely precise: "Somewhere a pane of glass falls. I hear its large fragments laugh, the small ones titter." For Malte, the sound of glass breaking is not a noise but a subtly organized sequence of sounds. Malte's problem, and the task he sets himself, is to find a coherent structure for the fragments of his self and his culture. The dissociated city of Paris is his location in the present; it is the place from which his mind probes his past. The characters Malte encounters in Paris, as well as the ones he remembers meeting in Petersburg or Venice, are all monads like himself.

Malte's attempts to integrate himself and the world of things in order to write might not succeed—the end of Rilke's novel is ambiguous, and puts any resolution off into an indefinite future—but he is sharply aware of the problems and works hard at trying to define them. Eliot's Prufrock, on the other hand, seems totally devoid of energy. He sees the isolated lives of others in the city as a projection of his own defeated life. Prufrock asks:

Shall I say, I have gone at dusk through narrow streets
And watched the smoke that rises from the pipes
Of lonely men in shirt-sleeves, leaning out of windows?[2]

In *The Waste Land* there is no single character like Prufrock to wander about in the dreary streets, but a kaleidoscopic series of disembodied voices, giving utterance to the shards of culture of which the modern city consists. This city is London. Eliot had originally had Dryden's London in mind as his literary model and counterpoint,[3] although in the course of the poem's crystallization "its center had become the urban apocalypse, the great City dissolved into a desert where voices sang from exhausted wells."[4]

The Waste Land is the epic of dissociated urban life in the earlier part of the twentieth century. The "unreal city" is the poem's central organizing metaphor, the center of imaginative and mythic power in an exhausted culture. The denizens of this city lead encapsulated, enervated lives. The poem's disembodied voices seem to emanate from one mind, but they all speak a bleak despair, from the voice which intones "unreal city" to the singsong line from the nursery rhyme, "London Bridge is falling down falling down falling down." The characters in the poem might be refugees from Thomson's "City of Dreadful Night," or later forms of the hollow urban characters in *Our Mutual Friend*. (Eliot had originally thought to call his poem "He Do the Police in Different Voices," a line from Dickens' novel.)

In Kafka's *Trial*, the city reflects the same vaporization of the significance of the individual as do Eliot's poems, but in different terms. In this novel the city consists of its institutions, rather than social encounters and cultural memories and fantasies: bank, boardinghouse, quasi-legal bureaucracy, cathedral. All these institutions belong together in some shadowy scheme of things, but they are completely unrelated to each other in the novel's sphere of everyday life. Joseph K. defines and measures himself completely in terms of these institutions, and not at all from some integral sense of himself as a person. Above all he seems to apply the model of the hierarchy of the bank, with which he is most familiar and most identified, to everything he is confronted with: an institutional model of subalterns and superiors, of venality, corruption, and arrogance. Even the sexual behavior of characters in *The Trial*, such as it is, shares the routine boredom, exhaustion, and despair of the secretary in *The Waste Land* and the wan erotic fantasies of Prufrock. This most intimate and vital human function fails of passion in these works. These devitalized and barely characterized individuals inhabit unreal cities which are, in their respective works, presented as incoherent fragments, randomly perceived. There are no sights from a steeple in these poems of Eliot or in Kafka's novel.

The Trial contains vivid descriptions of everyday urban life. Readers usually overlook them because of the anxiety aroused by Joseph K.'s abstract struggle with the Court, but they are important because they posit the existence of real communities in the world of this novel. (One of Kafka's largely unrecognized talents is his ability to show ordinary people at their day-to-day living, even if these scenes are susceptible of being interpreted in the light of Lefebvre's concept of "terrorism and everyday life."[5]) Here is one example, as K. is searching for the Court:

> He had thought that the house would be recognizable even at a distance by some sign which his imagination left unspecified, or by some unusual commotion before the door. But Juliusstrasse, where the house was said to be and at whose end he stopped for a moment, displayed on both sides houses almost exactly alike, high gray tenements inhabited by poor people. This being Sunday morning, most of the windows were occupied, men in shirt-sleeves were leaning there smoking or holding small children cautiously and tenderly on the window ledges. Other windows were piled high with bedding, above which the disheveled head of a woman would appear for a moment. People were shouting to one another across the street; one shout just above K.'s head caused great laughter. Down the whole length of the street at regular intervals, below the level of the pavement, there were little general grocery shops, to which short flights of steps led down. Women were thronging into and out of these shops or gossiping on the steps outside. A fruit hawker who was crying his wares to the people in the windows above, progressing almost as inattentively as K. himself, almost knocked K. down with his pushcart. A phono-

105

graph which had seen long service in a better quarter of the town began stridently to murder a tune.[6]

Joseph K. has blundered into a neighborhood community from which he is excluded: the community of Sunday-morning life in a residential city street. The narrator presents the scene as Joseph K. might visually perceive it, although K. is described as progressing "inattentively." The people pay no attention to him; there is no interaction or reaction on either side. Kafka seems to have derived this technique of contrasting an isolated protagonist with the community of an urban neighborhood from Dostoevsky's *Crime and Punishment*, but in *The Trial* the process is much more abstract. This is largely because the character of Joseph K. is much flatter than Raskolnikov, and not presented psychologically.

By focussing in this manner on individual characters separated from a community, writers make the outsider the focal point of urban culture—which is to say culture generally—and present the community more or less from the outsider's alienated viewpoint. As a reflection of the writer's attitude toward his culture, this focus on the outsider is a negative sign. Behind the writer's crystallizing expression of it, this perception is a reflection of an attitude widespread in the culture itself.

If we think back to Balzac's Rastignac and Dickens' Pip, we also find in them outsiders who are isolated in, and chastised by, the city. But they are bent on getting into the mainstream of the moral or social values of their societies, however they (or their authors) conceived of them. These protagonists are trying to escape from the isolation of provincial life by migrating to the city—only, of course, to be disillusioned once they get there. Later generations of characters were presented as city types to begin with, as the city in literature came to represent increasingly the feeling that modern culture was hollow. (It is worth repeating that this widespread attitude, commonly expressed in literature, did not correspond to the rapid economic and physical growth of real cities in the Western world in the later nineteenth and early twentieth centuries. The discrepancy reinforced the ambivalence of the city as a cultural sign.)

The high-water mark of the city as an emblem of cultural decay mirroring the decay of an isolated artist-figure was perhaps reached in Thomas Mann's *Death in Venice* (1911). In addition to the general appeal of Venice to nineteenth-century writers and painters, Mann also appeals, with virtuoso skill, to a specifically German network of associations Venice would have had for his contemporary readers.

Venice was a favorite topos of nineteenth-century English, French, and German art and literature. It was celebrated for its Romanticism, its exotic architecture, and its aesthetic qualities as a water-city. Venice lives in a quiet present, crumbling slowly; its glory as a center of trade and art lies in the distant past, which echoes into the present only through the monuments of its architecture. It became wealthy as the point of contact in trade between northern and western Europe and the near and far East. Mann uses this historical fact to give a psychological and philosophical underlay to his story: his Venice is the meeting-point of that northern and western Europe which is the home of the tense individual will and the Freudian ego and superego (exemplified in Aschenbach's earlier career) and the fatalistic Indian East, the source of Schopenhauer's cosmic Will as well as of the cholera, and the locale in the story of the Freudian unconscious—all of which catch up with the older Aschenbach. The half-Polish and half-mythical Tadzio, with his classical Greek aura, hovers in between as the visiting reigning divinity of Mann's Venice and Aschenbach's art.

In the German cultural tradition, Venice conjures up associations of erotic and homoerotic passion and the conflict between the repressed north of Europe and the licentious south.[7] The echoes of these associations in *Death in Venice* are many: Goethe's *Venetian Epigrams* of 1790, a Byronic mixture of personal travelogue and erotic dalliance; the *Sonnets from Venice* (1825) by August Graf Platen, an unhappy homosexual poet who died of an obscure infection contracted there. (Two of his poems, "Tristan" and "Venice," are specifically echoed in Mann's novella.) In addition, two of Mann's personal heroes had important links with Venice: It was Nietzsche's favorite city, about which he wrote several fine poems which place an existentially isolated character against its musical, exotic background, and Nietzsche's personal hero and cultural villain, Richard Wagner, wrote part of *Tristan and Isolde* in Venice (an opera on the theme of eroticism inspired in part by Wagner's discovery of Schopenhauer, who was yet another of Mann's personal deities). Wagner supplied the finishing touch for the background of Mann's novella by dying in Venice in 1883.

For the author and the reader of *Death in Venice*, the city evokes impressions of cultural decay and eroticism. Aschenbach sees Venice as a place to relax; he embodies the cultural decay and eroticism, without being consciously aware of them.[8] Aschenbach has become famous because his work expresses the spirit of the age. In reading Aschenbach's pages, the narrator says, one

> might doubt the existence of any other kind of heroism than the heroism born of weakness. And, after all, what kind could be truer to the spirit of the times? Gustave Aschenbach was the poet-spokesman of all those who labour at the edge of exhaustion; of the overburdened, of those who are already worn out but still hold themselves upright; of all our modern moralizers of accomplishment, with stunted growth and scanty resources, who yet contrive by skillful husbanding and prodigious

spasms of will to produce, at least for a while, the effect of greatness. There are many such, they are the heroes of the age. And in Aschenbach's pages they saw themselves; he justified, he exalted them, he sang their praise—and they, they were grateful, they heralded his fame.[9]

Aschenbach's flight from Munich to Venice is, on the surface of his mind, a desire for vacation, for a break in the intense strain of his work. He sees Venice, once he gets there, as a restful solitude paved with water. There is almost no dialogue in this novella; Aschenbach does not speak to his idol, Tadzio, although he has several opportunities to do so, and he has only the most cursory contact with the petty functionaries of the tourist's world. Aschenbach moves within the city and on the beach at its sea-edge, but he is dreamily detached, not aware—as the narrator makes the reader aware—of what is happening to him, or that the city is bodying forth his doom. His flight from Munich to Venice, from one city to another, is a flight from the scene of his artistic achievement in life towards the emblem of decay and death. Mann shows us not the young and struggling writer, but the elderly, declining one, whose ebbing vitality and increasing fatigue correspond to the devitalized characters of Eliot, Wilde, and Kafka.

Behind this ebbing of vitality from urban life in literature is the idea, frequently present only by implication, that a new, vital culture must arise to replace the old one. This is an extension of the apocalyptic idea of the destruction of a worn-out scheme of things. The general malaise which accompanied the sense of the doom of a civilization and the longing for a new order doubtless had much to do with the appeal of Fascism and Nazism in the 1920's and 1930's; both were notably urban phenomena dependent on the emotions of people as masses to thrive. (Nietzsche is sometimes implicated in this

109

development, but he was a polemical city-hater and individualist who castigated the estrangement caused by urban life.)[10]

The term "mass society" has become such a cliché that we do not quite realize how peculiar a concept it is. A mass of people differs from a crowd or a mob. "Crowd" is the most neutral of the three terms, a gathering of individuals with a common interest. "Mob," when not used casually, is pejorative; it refers to a disorderly crowd which can be violent or destructive. A "mass" of people connotes a large, undifferentiated bloc of people acting as a collective unit with a collective will. "Mass psychology" excludes the concept of the individual person entirely; indeed, it is often presented as its opposite. A person can retain his individuality in a crowd, or possibly even in a mob, but not in a mass. "Mass" is therefore a depersonalized concept, and also a negative one. It is applied to the lower classes of society, and the disappearance of an individual will in the collective emotion of the mass can easily become a metaphor for the submergence of "higher" civilized, rational thought into the "base" instincts of the mass. This figure, then, reflects the prejudice and fear of the upper classes of society toward the lower ones, or—Freud's terms seem metaphorically appropriate here—the fear of the organized ego toward the undifferentiated power of the id.

Although we associate the idea of mass society with a technological conception of culture, it seems to have originated earlier, probably with Edmund Burke's negative attitudes toward both the French Revolution and the rise of a new liquid-money class. The reduction of individuals to an abstract and mechanical function—"workers of the world," for example, or "The Revolt of the Masses"—was very much a creation of the nineteenth century. Robert Nisbet suggests that to see a human population as "the masses" is a subjective judgment not supported by objective or quantitative measurement. It

110

would not, he says, have arisen "in European writing had there not been the underlying vision of a once-organic, articulated, and rooted society converted by political and economic change into a mass society."[11]

The idea of people as masses plays on other deep cultural prejudices: the prejudice of the small town against the city, of the individual against technology. Raymond Williams points out that "there are in fact no masses; there are only ways of seeing people as masses. In an urban industrial society there are many opportunities for such ways of seeing. . . . What we see, neutrally, is other people, many others, people unknown to us. In practice, we mass them, and interpret them according to some convenient formula."[12] The concept of mass has created great mischief in urban sociology: "Because cities represent mass society, mass planning, bulldozing, leveling, and wholesale tearing-up of large areas is required to purge them."[13] (Baudelaire, in juggling the terms "multitude" and "solitude," had conceived of a multitude as a crowd; the concept of a mass of people was yet to come.) It now seems normal to us to think of city people as an urban mass; people who live in cities are very aware of rush hour and street-scene masses, and there is as well "the more general sociological fact that contemporary city life appears to provide few ways for seeing people as individuals."[14]

Presenting people as a mass instead of as a crowd seems to have begun in literature in the late nineteenth century with such scenes as Tolstoy's description of the battle of Borodino in *War and Peace* and Zola's habit of generalizing social description, as well as in scenes such as the rampaging miners in *Germinal*.[15] But the more general idea of mass and the concept of mass society is especially associated with the movement called Expressionism in painting and literature, which flourished in Germany before, during, and after the First World War. Literary expressionism attempted to re-establish a direct, basic commonality of urban mass experience, at the

111

fairly low level at which individuals share characteristics. (The contradiction was inherent in the beliefs and practices of the Expressionists.) A large part of this impulse was a reaction against the kind of overwrought neurotic individualism evident, for instance, in the novels of Thomas Mann and in Rilke's *Malte Laurids Brigge*. The result was either a very sophisticated naiveté or a generalized abstraction. Characters in plays are not named, but are labeled with their work or family functions: "cashier," "mother," "director," "men in tuxedos" (Georg Kaiser, *Von Morgens bis Mitternachts*). In a poem called "The God of the City" Georg Heym combines the presentation of city-dwellers as a mass with an apocalyptic vision of the destruction of the city by fire:

> He sits broadly on a block of houses.
> The winds camp black around his forehead.
> He gazes full of wrath to where, distant in loneliness,
> The last houses lose their way into the country.
> The idol's red belly shines from the evening,
> The great cities kneel around him.
> The monstrous number of church bells
> Surges up to him out of the sea of black towers.
>
> Like a Corybantic dance the music
> Of the millions drones loud through the streets.
> The chimney's smoke, the clouds of the factory
> Rise up to him, as haze blues from incense.
> The weather smolders in his eyebrows.
> The dark evening is drugged into night.
> The storms flap, gazing like vultures
> From his headhair, which bristles up in anger.
>
> He stretches his butcher's fist into the darkness.
> He shakes it. A sea of fire chases
> Through a street. And the firesmoke rages
> And eats it up, till late the morning dawns.[16]

This poem reads in some respects like Baudelaire's "Landscape," with a demonized vision of a wrathful god replacing the poet as gargoyle above the city. But Baudelaire's poem is built around the primacy of the individual poetic imagination, which first poeticizes the commercial and industrial city and then withdraws from it. Heym's poem, on the other hand, completely denies what Schopenhauer called the principle of individuation. The persona of the poet does not figure in the poem, and the "city" of the title is a collective appellation, echoed in the plural "cities" of the text itself. This city is seen in terms of its buildings; its people are mentioned only once, and then as mass celebrants of an orgiastic pagan rite, an indefinite large number in a qualifying genitive phrase.

Heym's god personifies the negative bias of a culture toward itself. The primitive mythic forces of wrath, night, storms, and destruction by fire—in short, the forces of chaos—are directed at man's central cultural object and symbol of order, the city. One might be tempted to read this poem as a description of the bombing of European cities during the Second World War, but Heym can only be called prescient: This poem was written in December, 1910, and Heym was drowned in a skating accident in 1912.

The principle of individuation is also weak in Biely's *St. Petersburg*, in which the writer's perspective also reduces people to a living but undifferentiated mass, a bloc which generates its own disconnected rhythms:

> The crowd of shoulders formed a cohesive and slowly moving mass. Alexander Ivanovich's shoulder glued itself to the mass and, obeying the impulse of the mass, moved upon the Nevsky Prospect. The bodies of those who were thrown upon the pavement were transformed into one general body, like grains of caviar. The pavements of the Nevsky formed a sandwich field where individual thought became part of the general thought of the polypedal creature which crawled along with it.

. . .

113

There were no individual persons on the Nevsky, but only a crawling, growling polypod, sprinkling forth a variety of voices, broken down into a variety of words; intermingling, the words wove themselves into phrases, meaningless phrases which hovered like black smoke over the Nevsky. And swelling against it, the Neva pressed against its massive cage of granite.[17]

This conception of the living mass as an amorphous polypod (and of the river as a caged beast) seems of a piece with the conception of the city itself as a place of shifting rhythms and ectoplasms rather than of stable objects and substantial characters. A process of abstracting amorphous shapes has replaced the mimetic representation of particulars.

Musil, in one of the most striking scenes in *The Man without Qualities*, achieves a powerful effect by bluntly opposing his alienated hero, Ulrich, to a mass which crystallizes in the square before Graf Leinsdorf's palace in Vienna. Ulrich, looking down from a window of the palace, is separated from the mass of people physically as well as mentally:

Ulrich had stepped to the window as the procession came up. Policemen marched along beside it at the edges of the streets and scattered bystanders out of the way like a cloud stirred up by the closed march-step. Here and there further on vehicles stood, already prevented from moving. The imperious stream flowed around them in boundless waves, on which one felt the dissolved spray of the bright faces dancing. As the first of the marchers came in sight of the palace, it seemed that some command moderated their step; a blocked wave ran backwards, the onpressing rows collided with each other, and an image arose which for a moment reminded of a muscle tensing before the blow. In the next moment this blow rushed through the air, looking strange enough, since it consisted of a cry of indignation, of which one saw the gaping mouths before one heard the sound. Blow upon blow opened the faces wide the moment they appeared, and since the shouting of those further away was drowned out by those who had in the meantime come nearer, by glancing into the distance one could see this mute spectacle constantly repeating itself.[18]

Like Hawthorne in "The Gray Champion," Musil emphasizes that the gathering of the mass paralyzes the normal functioning of the streets; it flows imperiously around the vehicles prevented from moving. But the larger effect of this scene depends on perspective: distance separates sight from sound, emotion from expression. The shouts arrive later than the mouths utter them, to the distant observer; thus he can see the phenomenon as a "spectacle" (*Schauspiel*), a theater piece. The separation of emotion from utterance expresses the novel's themes in several ways. Ulrich has been painfully aware from the beginning of the novel of his own dissociation and separation from the lives which swirl around him in the big city; this is a metaphor of his separation from social life itself. His reaction to the dissociated shouts of the mass is curious. He is violently and scornfully hostile, but he reacts to its kinesis with an involuntary physical movement of his own, which makes Graf Leinsdorf, who is in the room with him, think that Ulrich has cut himself on a sharp blade, "of which there was no possibility far and wide."

Ulrich's increasing depression is the theme of this critical series of chapters in *The Man without Qualities*. He wants to reorganize social life so that technology and feeling would not be at opposite poles of life—the legacy of the nineteenth century—but in harmony with each other. The massing of the people, whose passion has been aroused by ignorance and rumor, demonstrates to him the futility of his mission. The dissociated shouts are shouted at him, the metaphor of the muscle tensing for a blow and then striking out is aimed at him. Musil has concentrated the furious power of the city in this mindless mass and discharged it on the powerless thinking individual.

Later in this same sequence of chapters, Ulrich is shown walking home that night through the now deserted streets of the city. These streets were earlier too full to function as normal avenues of communication; now they are too empty. The theatrical metaphor of the mass scene is repeated in the emptiness: "One could have the feeling of action in this night as in a theater."[19] In this crass opposition between the streets overfilled by the depersonalized mass of his fellow citizens, and his own walk home through a paved solitude, Ulrich expresses his deepest feeling of dissociation from life, the feeling that "one was an appearance in this world; something which has an effect greater than it in itself is."[20]

This perception of city people as a depersonalized mass, whether by character, narrator, or author, introduces a new way of seeing into the literature of the city, as well as a new device for indicating the most extreme form of depersonalization: the individual is opposed no longer to a collection of other people grouped together as a community, but to the mass as a depersonalized animate object. Animate and inhuman at the same time that it is composed of people, the concept of human masses explodes the idea of community and society.

Nowhere City or Utopia?

O rising winter sun, pale wheatcolored wafer pasted
  against the sky between the buildings on
                14th Street,
visible against the girders on the 59th Street
                bridge, laden
  with cars locked into the morning holding patterns.
Having come first isolate above the greencold waves
  at Montauk, among the beach homes and
                empty shopping plazas. . .

—FREDERICK BUELL

In *The Secular City*, Harvey Cox traces the strain in contemporary Christianity back to the conflict inherent in the grafting of the Greek conception of the world as place—a spatial concept—onto the Hebrew conception of the world as essentially history, a process in time, "a series of events beginning with Creation and heading towards a consummation."[1] This dualism between secular space and religious time has been a mainspring of Western culture. Religious time dominated the European Middle Ages; the Renaissance rediscovered the excitement of secular space, and since then space and time have contended for dominance as the framework for our cultural outlook.

A quick sketch of this dualism in modern times points to a common thread running through some quite varied instances.[2] In the eighteenth century, the religious concept of time became generally secularized, although Defoe and Rousseau, among others, seem to continue using the opposition between a secular sense of space and a religious sense of time as a basic framework for their fiction. By conceiving of history as a rational progressive process in time, Hegel appropriated the religious idea and made history, for much of the nineteenth century, the religion of time. Time seemed to Schopenhauer a desperate problem to be overcome, and art the function of Western culture which enables man to do so and thus rejoin what Whitman was to call the "float."

Darwin's theory of natural selection, and Freud's theory of psychoanalysis, which traces the source of adult neuroses to early childhood, are both time-based, and Einstein revealed time to be the basic principle upon which space and matter depend. More recently, the temporal concept of entropy has been quite loosely borrowed from physics to justify the apparent running-down of Western civilization—an up-to-date and more sophisticated replay of Spengler's apocalyptic vision. Randomness and chance, which operate in time, have become important as physics, departing increasingly from Newtonian determinism, comes to a clearer understanding of how natural laws operate. Randomness and chance are prominent features of contemporary city literature: Sartre's *Nausea* is one case, and Pynchon's more rigorously scientific *Gravity's Rainbow* (in which the destruction of cities is a major theme) is another.[3]

Einstein's demonstration that time is a relative rather than a mechanically unvarying force was of a piece with the relativizing of perspective going on in the sciences and the arts at the end of the nineteenth century. In literature, as in psychology and philosophy, time was increasingly perceived as subjective and relative. It became a problem of inwardness,

118

of subjective duration, stream of consciousness, processes of memory. The emergence of modern concepts of myth and archetypes, and such ideas as the collective unconscious, the timeless Freudian unconscious, involuntary memory, and the belief in art as the bestower of immortality on the artist, can all be seen as metaphoric strategies designed in some sense to counter the increasing dominance of time in Western culture by positing a *nunc stans*, a static present, outside its power. Not accidentally, modern sociology was developed in the nineteenth century. It has been strongly marked as a science of space, which seeks to analyze local social processes in fixed habitats, while riven by the relativism of time, in which these same processes are seen as subject to constant change and changing judgments.

In our contemporary world, then, time operates as the cultural convention which dominates the way we look at the spatial world around us and the way we think about it. This places narrative literature, especially, in a paradoxical situation, for narrative fiction is for the reader a temporal medium which must create the illusion of events happening in space. It also, however, depends on a succession of spatial scenes to give the narrative the illusion of the passage of time. Up until the late eighteenth century this fact was accepted without difficulty as a convention of literature. The co-ordinates of time and space were used fairly matter-of-factly, even in the literature of fantasy, to locate action and character, aside from such prophetic sports as Sterne's *Tristram Shandy* and the novels of Jean Paul Richter. But beginning in the late eighteenth century writers such as Rousseau, Goethe, and Wordsworth began to emphasize the temporal in their prose and poetry, and to organize space in temporal terms. The context of this temporal organization was not universal, divine time but the time-span bounding the consciousness and the life of the individual. Spatial images in fiction and poetry became embedded in a prominent time-matrix.

119

Seen from this point of view, the image of the city in a literary work occupies a peculiar position. Since its conceptual as well as its empirical referent is a physical object in space, the word-city is an inherently spatial image. But this unavoidable association with spatiality conflicts in modern literature with the dominating convention of time. Perhaps this explains why so many cities in contemporary literature are etherealized or disembodied, like Biely's St. Petersburg, Musil's Vienna, or Eliot's London. This etherealization reduces their spatial presence so that they appear as dependencies of time; they become images which reflect transitoriness rather than stable corporeal places. Unlike their nineteenth-century counterparts of the realistic mode in literature, many of these semi-transparent cities are overtly fantasies rather than toponymical representations of real places. They are usually placed in a time-frame rather than a space-frame. Thus "Venice" in Proust's *In Search of Lost Time* has a name, but exists only by virtue of the narrator's imagined anticipation of it as a magic place. When he finally gets there, he is disappointed in what he finds; Venice is vital not in itself, but as a word which has animated the narrator's imagination. (In *Death in Venice* the city is bifocal: a geographical place on a time-journey for Aschenbach, a transparent, mythic place for the narrator.)

However, the city as a spatial object is so central to man's sense of cultural identity that to etherealize it is bound to meet with a resistance indicating anxiety. Perhaps this resistance arises from the basic biologic need of any living organism to be able to orient itself spatially in relation to its surroundings in order to insure its own survival. Being lost and being found are defined in terms of spatial reference, and there seems to be a strong physiological resistance, as well as a psychological one, to being disoriented. The reactions of Joseph K. in the first chapter of Kafka's *The Trial* to the dislocation of his normal routine and his landlady's apartment are a marvelous gloss on such disorientation. In nineteenth-century realistic novels the strong sense of place is a source of satisfaction to the reader, whatever dire events or people may occupy them; the absence of this strong sense of place in some twentieth-century novels—such as those of Robbe-Grillet and Sarraute—is disorienting and disquieting, however bland the characters or proceedings.

Our innate biological dependence on spatial orientation can be understood in an extended as well as a limited sense. Kevin Lynch points out that the environmental image "can serve as a general frame of reference within which the individual can act, or to which he can attach his knowledge. In this way it is like a body of belief, or a set of social customs: it is an organizer of facts and possibilities."[4]

If the environmental, or spatial, image is the city with its multifarious and conflicting associations, one can understand why it is so potent. The city as a spatial form presents both the image of a map and the image of a labyrinth: figures by which characters orient, but can also lose, themselves. Reflecting this inherent ambiguity, the image of the city functions as a nodal point of anxiety for the reader as well as for the characters. Anxiety is a strong thematic element in Leopold Bloom's wanderings around Dublin, or Kafka's K. wandering about the "village" beneath the castle,[5] or Rilke's Malte walking through the streets of Paris. The reader's response to this association of city and anxiety in the fictional character involves, it seems to me, his own subliminal apperceptions and anxieties.

As time became the prevalent convention in literature, literature generally began to lose its concern with formal shape, and spatial description was used less and less to evoke character and action. Formal shape is characteristic of a naturalistic, mimetic style: the art theorist Wilhelm Worringer suggested that such a style is characteristic of cultures which have in some way achieved an equilibrium between man and cos-

121

mos, but in a historical period of disharmony and disequilib-
rium, styles in art are non-organic and linear-geometric rather
than naturalistic.[6]

A poem by Brecht, "Of Poor B.B.," offers an apt example
of this linear-geometric style and the disembodied city:

1

I, Bertolt Brecht, came out of the black forests.
My mother moved me into the cities as I lay
Inside her body. And the coldness of the forests
Will be inside me until my dying day.

2

In the asphalt city I'm at home. From the very start
Provided with every last sacrament:
With newspapers. And tobacco. And brandy.
To the end mistrustful, lazy and content.

3

I'm polite and friendly to people. I put on
A hard hat because that's what they do.
I say: they are animals with a quite peculiar smell.
And I say: does it matter? I am too.

4

Before noon on my empty rocking chairs
I'll sit a woman or two, and with an untroubled eye
Look at them steadily and say to them:
Here you have someone on whom you can't rely.

5

Towards evening it's men that I gather around me
And then we address one another as 'gentlemen.'
They're resting their feet on my table tops

And say: things will get better for us. And I don't ask
    when.

6

In the grey light before morning the pine trees piss
And their vermin, the birds, raise their twitter and
    cheep.
At that hour in the city I drink up my glass, then throw
The cigar butt away and worriedly go to sleep.

7

We have sat, an easy generation
In houses held to be indestructible
(Thus we built those tall boxes on the island of
    Manhattan
And those thin aerials that amuse the Atlantic swell).

8

Of those cities will remain: what passed through them,
    the wind!
The house makes glad the eater: he clears it out.
We know that we're only tenants, provisional ones
And after us there will come: nothing worth talking
    about.

9

In the earthquakes to come, I very much hope
I shall keep my cigar alight, embittered or no
I, Bertolt Brecht, carried off to the asphalt cities
From the black forests inside my mother long ago.[7]

The power of this poem derives from the withdrawal of
meaning from the city as a human community located in space
while leaving it exposed to the apocalyptic process of time.
The city is disembodied, and the speaker is alienated both

123

from and in it, although he paradoxically calls it home. "Of Poor B.B." might well have been titled "Paved Solitude"; this anonymous, etherealized "asphalt city" provides the only definition of himself the speaker can give. Although the ironic title is personal, and the poem's mode confessional, this city is a sign, not a place. It does not have a name; it is both singular and plural. The only city named in the poem is "Manhattan," the myth-capital of the twentieth century, but it is not the city the speaker lives in, and even this "Manhattan" is presented in terms of estrangement and archaic language ("tall boxes," "*Eiland*").[8]

Similarly, three of the poem's nine stanzas imply a house the speaker lives in, but the house is not mentioned. The house, like the city, is a negative presence, a sign of estrangement, the exact opposite of the concept of the house as a home, "one of the greatest powers of integration for the thoughts, memories and dreams of mankind."[9]

Although the speaker lives in one city, he has a collective consciousness of cities: the already general location in the second stanza ("in the asphalt city") is broadened in the final stanza to "in the asphalt cities," and in the penultimate stanza the reduction of cities to mute objects rather than the home of man is also plural. The disembodied city/cities in which the speaker is "at home" are the appropriate homes of "an easy generation."

This emptiness of the speaker's urban present is contrasted with the mysterious past of the "black forests" with which the poem begins and ends. Like the cities of his present, these unknown forests of his past are also disembodied ("the black forests" instead of the geographically specific "Black Forest"). His whole life is expressed in these etherealized plurals: "people," "a woman or two," "men," "the pines," "boxes," "aerials," "earthquakes." The city, as a basic emblem of community, ought to be the glue that binds the speaker, his past, his fellow-human beings into a meaningful society, but this

124

glue has come unstuck, leaving only the pitiless tyranny of time to dominate the poem. The climax of the poem is a vision of destruction in future time.

The time process of this poem, from prenatal wilderness to the vision of the apocalyptic destruction of the city, parallels Oswald Spengler's cycle of the decay of civilization from the peak of primitive agrarianism to the decadence of the modern megalopolis.[10] In progressing from the expulsion from a kind of Eden into a sinful world slated for doom, both Brecht and Spengler are, of course, following a Biblical pattern. (This might have had something to do with the vast popularity of Spengler's pseudo-scientific gloom.)

Hugo's "Arch of Triumph," written nearly a hundred years before Brecht's poem, also dealt with a city subjected to the vision of apocalypse at a future time. But specificity of place had been the heart of Hugo's poem. Paris and its famous monuments provided the mythic referents; the poet provided the vision of apocalypse. In Hugo's poem the city was the center of the universe, as it had been in early cultures; the speaker was an anonymous, prophetic voice, speaking with some kind of visionary authority. In Brecht's poem the city is both anonymous and amorphous; the speaker is ironic and individualizes himself. This "Bertolt Brecht" is speaking not as a visionary but as an imprecator.

Antoine Roquentin in Sartre's *Nausea* is another imprecator in the Brechtian vein. A fairly direct descendant of Rilke's Malte Laurids Brigge—but, unlike Malte, filled with self-loathing—Roquentin is another dissociated, mocking individual baring his teeth at the decayed civilization of faceless cities:

> I am afraid of cities. But you mustn't leave them. If you go too far you come up against the vegetation belt. Vegetation has crawled for miles towards the cities. It is waiting. Once the city is dead, the vegetation will cover it, will climb over the stones, grip them, search them, make

125

them burst with its long black pincers; it will blind the holes and let its green paws hang over everything. You must stay in the cities as long as they are alive, you must never penetrate alone this great mass of hair waiting at the gates; you must let it undulate and crack all by itself. In the cities, if you know how to take care of yourself, and choose the times when all the beasts are sleeping in their holes and digesting, behind the heaps of organic debris, you rarely come across anything more than minerals, the least frightening of all existants.

I am going back to Bouville. The vegetation has only surrounded three sides of it. On the fourth side there is a great hole full of black water which moves all by itself. The wind whistles between the houses.[11]

This anti-hero, whose name means "old beau" or "old fogey," clings to this city whose name suggests "Mudville." In his surrealistic vision, the mineral city with its jungle beasts fights off the devouring jungle and the senseless ocean. One might regard this vision as an externalization of Roquentin's self-loathing and alienation; what is curious about the vision is that the city, which is its centerpiece, is what Roquentin feels he must hang on to. Like Brecht's "Poor B.B.," Roquentin is condemned to be at home in the asphalt cities.

The disembodied city may have achieved its apotheosis in Italo Calvino's *Invisible Cities*, a narrative somewhere between novel and poem. Given the inherent spatiality of the city, Calvino's title amounts to an oxymoron, a contradiction in terms on which the writer plays like a virtuoso fiddler on his instrument. These cities are "invisible" because they exist only as inventions of the imagination of the narrator, Marco Polo. By this device Calvino underscores the fact that word-cities exist not in space, but in narrative time. Marco Polo is describing his cities to the Emperor Kublai Khan, who is listening to the young Venetian recount his "travels" through the emperor's vast, unreal, and crumbling empire, known to this ruler only through hearsay. Polo's cities are verbal constructs invented to amuse this Emperor, who sounds as if Yeats' Byzantium might also be one of his territories.

"Cities are made of desires and fears," Polo tells the emperor;[12] projected shadows of man's two basic emotions. The cities of this narrative are divided into eleven kinds, each of which is further fragmented by being presented in discontinuous sections: cities and memory, cities and desire, cities and signs, thin cities, trading cities, cities and eyes, cities and names, cities and the dead, cities and the sky, continuous cities, and hidden cities. The capricious categories are as transparent as the cities they enclose, which reflect not the places themselves but the imaginer "seeing" them as he tells about or invents them.

(Fantasy and science sometimes echo each other in unexpected ways. A sociologist, listing some of the varieties of real cities, sounds like Calvino: "There are specialized cities: for sin, . . . for resort living, for old folks, for conventions, . . . There are towns which have had glorious histories but have dim futures; towns with minor histories and seemingly little future. There are cities which consider themselves rivals of certain nearby cities, and ones which rival distant cities. There are cities which are run by outsiders, and ones which are governed by insiders—by old elites or by new elites.")[13]

The cities in *Invisible Cities* all bear female names. However, they seem to be the same city, perhaps Polo's native Venice (*Venezia*), described in different guises and disguises. The typing of cities as female recalls on the one hand Mumford's depiction of early settlements as containers, symbolizing the female principle, and on the other hand Balzac's Paris and Angoulême, cities also under the sign and domination of woman. (Women in Balzac's cities are the divinities of place, the sacred goddesses whom his upward-striving hunter-he-

127

roes must both propitiate and conquer in order to possess *le monde*.)

But however transparent and disembodied Calvino's cities are, the problem of the city as a physical object in space will not go away, even for him. It remains a paradox which is a constant source of mental gymnastics in *Invisible Cities*. The art of this book is to describe these cities; but to describe them is to make them visible by conjuring their qualities as existing in space. In accord with the modern temper, this fugitive spatiality is located within the inexorability of time, revealed as the meaningless process of history. The emperor, whose shadowy empire in space is crumbling in time, owns an atlas containing all the maps of all the cities of the past, the present, and the future. This atlas "reveals the form of cities that do not yet have a form or a name"[14]—in other words, that do not exist. An atlas identifies topographic entities by their shape, more specifically by their boundary shapes, or outlines. Name and shape confer identity: It is as if the genes of the names combined with the genes of spatial shape in a spooky heredity of cities. According to this genetic trace, the shapes and names of old cities determine the shape of new ones with the same names.

There is the city in the shape of Amsterdam, a semi-circle facing north, with concentric canals . . . ; there is the city in the shape of York, set among the high moors, walled, bristling with towers; there is the city in the shape of New Amsterdam known also as New York, crammed with towers of glass and steel on an oblong island between two rivers, with streets like deep canals. . . .

The catalogue of forms is endless: until every shape has found its city, new cities will continue to be born. When the forms exhaust their variety and come apart, the end of cities begins. In the last pages of the atlas there is an outpouring of networks without beginning or end, cities in the shape of Los Angeles, in the shape of Kyōto-Ōsaka, without shape.[15]

Lurking in the depths of Calvino's playful reduction of the essence of cities to their shape is the notion that shape is the means by which we recognize things in the world of space. We individualize, and evoke, cities by referring to their shapes, or—since we do not often see them as a whole from the air, which this implies—to characteristic boundary shapes, like water edges. (Boundary edges of and within cities are basic to the orientation of their inhabitants.)[16] Recognition of shape is vital to the identification of cities. This might explain why cities built on islands, or by rivers, lakes, or oceans, have special appeal to the imagination, in addition to the archetypal associations of bodies of water; such cities have dramatic boundaries as points of orientation, a sharp outline as opposed to a diffuse one. As an observer looking at the shape of New York marked off by "its almost incomparable river," Henry James saw "the huge jagged city . . . , in her long leanness, where she lies looking up at the sky in the manner of some colossal hair-comb turned upward and so deprived of half its teeth that the others, at their uneven intervals, count doubly as sharp spikes."[17]

The absence of shape in the form of orienting landmarks is a major problem for a person trying to define a real city or navigate within it.[18] If shape makes individual cities recognizable, urban shapelessness is a form of disorder expressing anxiety and loss of coherence, and symbolizing the anonymous randomness of contemporary life. In The Nowhere City, Alison Lurie plays on the notorious shapelessness of Los Angeles to satirize the corresponding shapelessness of its patterns of middle-class living.

The concept of shape—usually in the form of shapelessness—plays a large role in contemporary urban sociology. Barbara Ward uses it as a metaphor to describe the modern

129

industrial city as "the unintended city," which has been "not so much planned for human purposes as simply beaten into some sort of shape by repeated strokes from gigantic hammers—the hammer of technology and applied power, the overwhelming drive of national self-interest, the single-minded pursuit of economic gain."[19] Sociologists generally prefer to talk about "megalopolis," "conurbation," or "commutershed" rather than "city." Obliterating the shape of the city by extending it to include a diffuse amount of territory beyond it is a way of defining the contemporary situation of the city by its shapelessness. But these terms might represent more a projection of cultural attitudes than a neutral description of realities. This preference for abolishing the shape of the city seems to imply a de-mythification of the city of monuments which has for so long expressed positive as well as negative attitudes toward culture.

When planners speak of rationalizing urban sprawl, they have until recently tended to think in terms of "organic deconstruction" of the central city core,[20] which would be replaced by smaller outflung clusters of homes, shopping, and industries, all rationally organized along rational transportation networks. The coiled energy of the spatially untidy supercity would, according to this now faded way of thinking, yield to an idealized spatial conception of groups of smaller communities, more supervillages than cities, and totally without the monuments or mythic energy of traditional cities.

Shape is a spatial concept. Even more central to sociological thinking is the organic metaphor, in which cities are conceived of in the same terms of growth and decline which apply to plants and animals. This is a temporal concept. In *The Culture of Cities*, for instance, Lewis Mumford appropriates the concept of *Abbau* ("un-building," as he calls it; devolution, deconstruction) from biology.[21] He applies it to his conception of the city as an organic entity which, like a biological organism, develops from a simple to an overcomplicated state and then devolves back to a simpler structure. (In biology the process is not so schematic; evolution and devolution can be going on in different parts of the same organism at the same time.)

As a temporal metaphor applied to the city, *Abbau* subordinates spatial organization (form, structure) to time (process). A metaphor, however, is an analogy, not an equation, and a city is not an organism: It is an inanimate spatial object to which the temporal laws of biological process do not really apply. Urban sociology, which is saturated with this metaphor, frequently finds itself in difficulty over it: "Thought and speech about cities are replete with temporal imagery," writes one American urban specialist. "Cities are represented as oriented toward the past, the present, or the future; . . . American cities frequently are characterized according to a future-oriented growth model ('expanding,' 'increasing,' or 'progressing') or an inverse growth model ('declining' or 'decreasing')." This critic notes too the use of biological metaphor: "The very terms used to describe city development are borrowed from the language of human development. For decades, Chicago has been described as 'adolescent,' but Milwaukee, which is about the same age, tends to be described as middle-aged and settled."[22]

Oswald Spengler pushes the organic-temporal metaphor to absurdity. He sees the modern megalopolis as a sterile end-stage ("intellect") in the growth and decay of civilization which began with the rural peasant ("soul"): "The Wheel of Destiny rolls on to its end; the birth of the City entails its death. Beginning and end, a peasant cottage and a tenement-block are related to one another as soul and intellect, as blood and stone."[23]

To see cities temporally by means of a biological analogy raises questions. "When does a city stop being represented as . . . young and become adolescent, why, and by whom? How long can a city exist without being regarded as old, or

131

even middle-aged? . . . What happens to temporal symbolism when a city is invaded by new waves of immigrants: is it conceived to be the same city, a different one, and in what degree, and by whom?"[24]

Robert Nisbet discusses this phenomenon more broadly as "the problem of motion" in viewing social development.[25] The imposition of the organic metaphor of birth, flourishing, and death onto nonorganic phenomena is a way of organizing a simple sequence of events into a hierarchy of values. As applied to the city the organic metaphor, with its emphasis on becoming rather than being, seems to be an attempt to reduce the city's irreducible occupation of space—concrete, stone, brick, and asphalt—to a shadowy and transient presence, which is more in keeping with the temporal orientation of our culture.

The stubborn spatiality of the city is perhaps best epitomized by its monuments, which are deeply rooted in the social and the individual mind: Wordsworth's "ships, towers, domes, theatres, and temples," Hugo's Notre Dame, King Kong's Empire State Building. At the beginning of Kafka's novel *America*, the Statue of Liberty is seen standing at the entrance to New York harbor and the New World with an upraised sword in her hand instead of her torch. Kafka, who never saw the statue except in pictures, knew what he was doing; anyone who examines it closely will see that the statue's posture is indeed aggressive, and that the sword would actually fit its stance better. One surmises that the symbolism intended by the sculptor of an aggressive statue holding a torch instead of a sword was meant to symbolize energy turned from aggression to the light of peace and knowledge. This monument, strikingly fixed in space at the entrance to New York harbor, expresses the future-oriented idealism of an entire nation. The statue itself has become a mythic object and a symbol of the United States. As we look at the statue today, we are impressed in a different way by the aggressive posture culminating in the torch of light: Perhaps this very powerful statue has seized the public imagination so strongly because it is, among other things, a monument to ambivalence.

The city itself is the most monumental of monuments. An urban expert comments on the new capital city that Nigeria is about to build in a remote rural area that a national capital "bears the symbolic torch for the entire nation—the image the chosen city creates is a powerful factor in national status and internal self-conception."[26] The dispersed city, diffused with its suburbs over a large amorphous area, is the closest that American (and more recently European) society has come to *Abbau*, but the dispersed city has signally failed to give rise to meaningful monuments or a meaningful culture. Central-city cores, even chaotic ones, remain the magnets for those things which give meaning to civilization. In discussing this problem, Mumford observes that "spatial concentration has an essential part to play in psychological focus."[27]

But most of the urban monuments of our time are depersonalized, like modern skyscrapers and much of modern life. The resulting spatial malaise is the subject of an article by Suzannah Lessard on New York's glass-curtain skyscrapers.[28] The author's point of view is that of an aesthetic moralist; her argument is especially interesting in the context of this chapter because of the way in which it is cast in temporal terms although its subject is urban space. She presents the unadorned architecture of twentieth-century skyscrapers as a protest against the ornamental Beaux-Arts style which preceded it. As not infrequently happens in cultural matters, a change in style became a moral judgment: the new bare style of architecture was proclaimed as true and honest as against the falseness and hypocrisy of its predecessor. Now that New York has entirely too many of these plain skyscrapers, and we are no longer culturally hostile to Beaux-Arts style, the

133

anomalies and deficiencies of the glass-curtain box style for tall buildings are becoming apparent.

The author places the history of architecture in another kind of time-frame as well. From the late eighteenth to the twentieth century, she points out, technological invention in structural engineering was a great stimulus for architecture, both aesthetically and as a way of demonstrating a new freedom and power. At a measured pace, architects were "working on the frontier of technological possibilities."[29] But then technology speeded up rapidly, and its glamor fled to other areas than the construction of buildings; structural engineering was left far behind. This valuation of spatial objects—buildings—as primarily functions of time rather than place is a curious expression of the value of impermanence which attaches to glass-curtain skyscrapers and serves as a locus for cultural ambivalence. Lessard cites one architect as saying that these buildings "would never become ruins, because as soon as they had outlived their purpose they would be dismantled, . . . 'These buildings are like Erector sets,' he said. 'All you have to do is unbolt them. I have seen a whole façade put up in a day. What goes up in a day can come down in a day.' "[30]

Lessard notes that the ambivalence aroused by these temporary monuments has found expression in contemporary writers. (We have already seen Brecht's "tall boxes of the island Manhattan.") "American writers," she says, "have lately taken to portraying modern architectural landscapes in an advanced state of decay—the jungle conquering the machine."[31] In Walker Percy's *Love in the Ruins*, Kurt Vonnegut's *Slapstick*, and Joan Didion's *A Book of Common Prayer*, Lessard points out that disintegration is seen not as distressing, but as an improvement: "What had been destroyed is seen as having been horrid in the first place. . . . The ruined modern architecture described in these novels really serves not as a warning but as the fulfillment of a wish: an imaginary killing of something that is not dead at all and is hated . . . for its very aliveness."[32]

Finally, Lessard makes a shrewd observation about the obsession of contemporary culture with time: "The most distressing aspect of the self-consuming culture has always been that, while nothing much lasts, or even seems worth keeping, the process of impermanence itself endures, with newness endlessly distracting attention from cultural thinness. [Rilke had made the same point fifty years earlier in the *Tenth Duino Elegy*.] An image of modern architecture in ruins enables a writer to take away the magic of constant renewal and, by showing what is left without this magic, demonstrate the innate worthlessness underneath."[33]

In our modern Western cities we live in space but think in time. The instability of our spatial surroundings seems not so much a fact in itself as evidence of a temporal process of decline and decay. We see spatial structures as ephemeral rather than as monuments, symbols of the permanent. This peculiar situation has been brilliantly captured by Gabriel García Marquez in *One Hundred Years of Solitude*, a hymn to time in the form of an apparent family history, in which time creates the illusion of space for the history to happen in: principally the half-real, half-fantastic, wholly imaginary village (later town) of Macondo. At the end of this novel the metaphor of the city occurs as pure image, disengaged from any specific referent. The last survivor is reading of his family's mysterious bloodline through time in the parchments of Melquíades as the wind destroys the town around him: "Macondo was already a fearful whirlwind of dust and rubble being spun about by the wrath of the biblical hurricane when Aureliano skipped eleven pages so as not to lose time with facts he knew only too well, and he began to decipher the instant that he was living, deciphering it as he lived it, prophesying himself in the act of deciphering the last page of the parchments, as if he were looking into a speaking mirror. . . . Before reaching the final line, however, he had already understood that he would never leave that room, for it was foreseen that the city of mirrors (or mirages) would be wiped out by the wind and exiled from the memory of men at the precise moment when Aureliano Babilonia would finish deciphering the parchments, . . ."[34] To what does "the city of mirrors (or mirages)" refer? Mirrors are reflecting objects, mirages the unreal reflections; the city is a purposeful organization in space—here of mirrors or mirages. Macondo, the town of the story, might be one metaphoric mirror in this city of mirrors. Others might be literature generally, this novel, the mind of the character Aureliano, or the mind of Marquez's reader. (As Aureliano is reading his parchments, the reader of *One Hundred Years of Solitude* is simultaneously reading Marquez's "parchments" in which Aureliano is reading. . . .)

Fugitive past, fugitive present, fugitive future: conceived as subservient to time, the city as an image can consist only of mirrors or mirages, which constantly refract and reflect shifting lights and angles in time. In these last pages the spatial scenes of Marquez's novel are all swept away by a final apocalypse of time, the "biblical hurricane," and it is the peculiar use of the city image which expresses the annihilation of this created world. Marquez's ending is an extravagant intensification of Walter Benjamin's statement that "the true image of the past *flits* by. Only as an image can the past, which flashes up only to disappear for ever at the moment of recognition, be captured."[35]

CONCLUSION

Paterson lies in the valley under the Passaic Falls
its spent waters forming the outline of his back. He
lies on his right side, head near the thunder
of the waters filling his dreams! Eternally asleep,
his dreams walk about the city where he persists
incognito. Butterflies settle on his stone ear.

—WILLIAM CARLOS WILLIAMS, *Paterson*

The constant which underlies the image of the city in literature seems to be, in different guises, the ambivalence the city has embodied throughout the history of European and American culture. From a reasonable point of view there can be no question of the overwhelmingly positive contributions of the city to Western civilization, whose culture the city defines, contains, and transmits. But the city has also been a totem for attitudes, feelings, and beliefs outside the realm of reason. As an emblem of these other forces, it has represented, with remarkable constancy, antithetical feelings which seem to be irreconcilable: order and disorder, mighty heart and paved solitude, Jerusalem and Babylon, nowhere city and utopia. However unresolved these conflicting attitudes toward the city have been, and whatever stresses they have produced or expressed, their presence has enormously enriched Western culture.

The art of literature, by imposing the imaginative order of its conventions on the disorder of life, might be the only realm in which these paradoxes can be encompassed. The conventions of literature are the medium of understanding between an artist and his audience, and through them between a culture and its people. The conventions of sociology and psychology have been developed on the linear, sequential model of the natural sciences, but those of literature can express many different things at once, and this may be the only way that the tangled complexities of the city can be captured at all.

In *The Tower of Babel*, Ludovico Quaroni has summed up the dilemma posed by the city, which he views on the one hand as an ideal abstract representation of the cosmic order, and on the other as a real place in which people act out the fitful and untidy dramas of everyday life. He opposes the Renaissance ideal of the city to the modern reality:

> The same axis passes through and symmetrically divides a building and the street which leads from the gate of the city and proceeds into the country, continuing as far as infinity the central idea of the finite building. Thus the city, like its very architecture, is organized according to a rigid, simple hierarchy of values. But the human dimension amalgamates everything and reduces the contrasts, humanizing and intellectualizing monumentality itself.

> The modern city, however, is a different one, which moves independently of these utopias. Far from intellectual extrapolations, it develops from tortuous medieval models toward the abstraction of the busily involved architect. Opposed to the universal, geometric, unitary, closed and finite, simple and humane perfection of the fantastic city of the dreamers is the entirely different empirical city of the entrepreneurs, which, far removed from aesthetic demands, transforms and expands the city

which already exists: The speculation of ideas collides with the speculation of actions.[1]

In this very modern view, the Renaissance ideal of the city is presented in terms of fixed spatial relationships embodying an ideal cosmic order; the dynamic modern city is presented in terms of action in time.

Two passages from contemporary writers bear witness to Quarino's opposition of the claims of the ideal city and the demands of the real one. The passages represent opposing viewpoints, but both visualize the city in strongly spatial terms. Calvino's *Invisible Cities* contains the following exchange:

"What meaning does your construction have?" he asks. "What is the aim of a city under construction unless it is a city? Where is the plan you are following, the blueprint?"

"We will show it to you as soon as the working day is over; we cannot interrupt our work now," they answer.

Work stops at sunset. Darkness falls over the building site. The sky is filled with stars. "There is the blueprint," they say.[2]

Donald Barthelme's story "City Life" contains the following rumination:

"Ramona thought about the city.

"—I have to admit we are locked in the most exquisite mysterious muck. This muck heaves and palpitates. It is multi-directional and has a mayor. To describe it takes many hundreds of thousands of words. Our muck is only a part of a much greater muck—the nation-state—which is itself the creation of that muck of mucks, human consciousness."[3]

These opposing views of the city, as reflections of the cosmic order and as muck ("a moist, sticky mixture, especially of mud and filth"—*American Heritage Dictionary*) constitute, taken together, an unresolved and perhaps unresolvable ambivalence. When a writer places this ambivalence in a setting in which European-American values collide with those of other cultures, the result is to awaken for the reader the deep fears and desires underlying all culture, those powerful emotions about which Freud speculated in *Civilization and Its Discontents* and *Totem and Taboo*.

In his novel *A Bend in the River*, V. S. Naipaul has skillfully orchestrated the anxieties arising from these feelings around the figure of an outsider living in a large town in a newly independent African country. The town, a regional market and trading center, expands and contracts in size according to political vicissitudes. It is dependent on the brutal and unpredictable power of the distant, undefined capital. Culturally, the town is the focal point at which the foreign values of outside culture (in this case post-colonial European) collide with the quite different tribal rhythms and patterns of village life in the surrounding bush. The villagers of the bush, when they come to the town, are as uprooted and lost as is the narrator, who comes from another African country but whose family and culture are Indian.

Throughout the novel, this town bodies forth the menacing anxieties felt by the narrator as well as the people of the region. For both narrator and natives, the town is the only locus of contemporary self-identity, but a foreign and alien one. In describing how the struggle for independence had unleashed the fear and anger of the inhabitants of the region, the narrator reports that the people, having been abused by Arabs and other Africans as well as Europeans, refused to accept the rule of the newly independent government in the distant capital, and in instinctive rage rose up and destroyed the town.

If the movement had been more reasoned, had been less a movement of simple rejection, the people of our region might have seen that the town at the bend of the river was theirs, the capital of any state they might set up. But they had hated the town for the intruders who had ruled in it and from it; and they had preferred to destroy the town rather than take it over.

Having destroyed their town, they had grieved for it. They had wished to see it a living place again. And seeing it come to a kind of life again, they had grown afraid once more.

They were like people who didn't know their own mind.[4]

NOTES

Preface

1. As summarized by E. H. Gombrich in: *Art and Illusion: A Study in the Psychology of Pictorial Representation* (Princeton: Princeton University Press, Bollingen Series XXXV, 5, 2nd ed., 1961), p. 280.

2. *Ibid., passim,* esp. pp. 86-90.

3. Max Weber, *The City,* tr. and ed. Don Martindale and Gertrud Neuwirth (New York: The Free Press, 1958), p. 83.

4. In *Totem and Taboo* Freud, using the anthropological observations and theories of Frazer, Smith, Wundt *et al.,* demonstrates the power of totemism and its connections—psychological as well as historical—to ambivalent impulses of desire and prohibition in the clan and in the individual.

Chapter I

1. *The Anatomy of Criticism* (Princeton: Princeton University Press, 1957), p. 346.

2. *The Idea of a Town: The Anthropology of Urban Form in Rome, Italy, and the Ancient World* (Princeton: Princeton University Press, 1976), p. 24. See also: Ludovico Quaroni, *La Torre di Babele* (Padova: Marsilio Editori, 1967), esp. pp. 178-213.

3. Robert Park *et al., The City* (Chicago: University of Chicago Press, 1967 [1925]), p. 1.

4. *Cosmos and History: The Myth of the Eternal Return,* transl. Willard R. Trask (New York: Harper and Row, Harper Torchbooks, 1959), p. 10.

5. *Ibid.,* p. 12.

6. Rykwert, p. 12.

7. *Ibid.,* pp. 25ff.

8. *Ibid.,* p. 35.

9. *Ibid.,* p. 174.

10. *Ibid.*

11. *Ibid.*, p. 59.

12. *Ibid.*, p. 72.

13. Jacques Ellul, *The Meaning of the City*, transl. Dennis Pardee (Grand Rapids: William B. Eerdmans, 1970), pp. 9-10.

14. *La Cité antique* (Paris, 1880), pp. 198-199. Quoted in Rykwert, p. 30.

15. Rykwert, pp. 196ff.

16. *Ibid.*, p. 190.

17. "The Origins and Development of Cities in the Near East," in *Janus: Essays in Ancient and Modern Studies*, ed. Louis L. Orlin (Ann Arbor: Center for Co-ordination of Ancient and Modern Studies, University of Michigan, 1975), p. 8.

18. In *The Poems of John Dryden*, ed. John Sargeant (London: Geoffrey Cumberledge/Oxford University Press, 1910), p. 18.

19. See Robert Nisbet, *Sociology as an Art Form* (New York: Oxford University Press, 1976), p. 32; Harvey Cox, *The Secular City*, rev. ed. (New York: Macmillan, 1968), chs. 1 and 2, and Terence Charles Stewart, compiler, *The City as an Image of Man* (London: Latimer Press, 1970).

20. *The Image of the City* (Cambridge, Mass.: The M.I.T. Press, 1960), pp. 1-2.

21. R. Richard Wohl and Anselm L. Strauss, "Symbolic Representation and the Urban Milieu," in *American Journal of Sociology*, Vol. LXIII, No. 5, March, 1958, pp. 523-532; p. 524.

22. *Ibid.*, p. 527.

23. *The American City Novel* (Norman: University of Oklahoma Press, 1954), p. 11.

24. *Homer and the Homeric Tradition* (New York: W. W. Norton, 1958), p. 27.

25. *European Literature and the Latin Middle Ages*, transl. Willard R. Trask (New York: Harper and Row, 1953), p. 157.

26. Citron, *La Poésie de Paris dans la littérature française de Rousseau à Baudelaire* (Paris: Les Éditions de Minuit, 1961); Williams, *The Country and the City* (New York: Oxford University Press, 1973).

27. Wohl and Strauss, p. 527.

28. *Ibid.*, p. 531.

29. "Psychology and Form," in *Counterstatement* (Berkeley: University of California Press, 1968), p. 36.

30. Gaston Bachelard, *The Poetics of Space*, transl. Maria Jolas (Boston: Beacon Press, 1969), pp. xiii, 33, xix.

31. *The Rise of the Novel* (Berkeley: University of California Press, 1957), p. 14.

32. *Ibid.*, pp. 12, 13.

33. *Ibid.*, p. 15.

34. Two interesting studies which approach this problem from different directions are: Donald Fanger, *Dostoevsky and Romantic Realism* (Chicago: University of Chicago Press, Phoenix Books, 1967) and Richard Sennett, *The Fall of Public Man: On the Social Psychology of Capitalism* (New York: Vintage Books, 1978).

35. (Bloomington: Indiana University Press, 1969), pp. 79-80.

36. *Der Mann ohne Eigenschaften*, in *Gesammelte Werke in Neun Bänden*, ed. Adolf Frisé (Reinbek bei Hamburg: Rowohlt Verlag, 1978), Vol. 1, pp. 11-12.

37. Transl. and ed. James Strachey (New York: W. W. Norton, 1962).

38. *Ibid.*, pp. 15-16.

39. *Ibid.*, pp. 17-18.

40. *Ibid.*, p. 18; Freud's emphasis.

41. *The Life and Work of Sigmund Freud* (New York: Basic Books, 1955), Vol. 2, pp. 16-18. Freud himself talks about his obsession with Rome in *The Interpretation of Dreams*, transl. and ed. James Strachey (New York: Avon Books, 1965), pp. 226-227 and n.

42. *The City in History* (New York: Harcourt, Brace, and World, 1961), p. 16.

43. *Civilization and Its Discontents*, pp. 70-71.

44. *Ibid.*, pp. 80-91; p. 91.

45. Mumford, p. 46.

46. *The Intellectual versus the City: From Thomas Jefferson to Frank Lloyd Wright* (New York: New American Library, 1962), pp. 13-14.

47. *Art and Illusion*, pp. 68-69.

48. *Ibid.*, p. 71.

49. (London: Oxford University Press, 1964), *passim*. See also Keats' ode "To Solitude."

50. *Oeuvres complètes* (Paris: Éditions Gallimard, Bibliothèque de la Pléiade, 1961), pp. 243-244.

51. "Das Paris des Second Empire bei Baudelaire: III. Das Moderne," in *Charles Baudelaire: Ein Lyriker im Zeitalter des Hochkapitalismus*, ed. Rolf Tiedemann (Frankfurt/Main: Suhrkamp Verlag. suhrkamp taschenbuch wissenschaft 47, 1974), p. 82.

52. *Everyday Life in the Modern World*, transl. Sacha Rabinovitch (New York: Harper and Row, 1971), p. 183.

Chapter II

1. For an interesting if summary discussion of Wordsworth's London, see Max Byrd, *London Transformed: Images of the City in the Eighteenth Century* (New Haven: Yale University Press, 1978), pp. 119-156.

2. *The Norton Anthology of English Literature*, ed. M. H. Abrams *et al.* (New

York: W. W. Norton, 1962), Vol. 2, p. 127n., and Mary Moorman, *William Wordsworth, A Biography* (Oxford: Clarendon Press, 1957-65), Vol. I, p. 563.

3. *Le monde comme il va*, in *Romans et contes*, ed. Henri Bénac (Paris: Garnier Frères, 1949), pp. 66-80.

4. See Mumford, *The City in History*, pp. 29-35, Rykwert, *The Idea of a Town*, Ch. I, and my discussions of Hugo and Pushkin.

5. See Watt, *Rise of the Novel*, p. 28.

6. *The City in History*, p. 7.

7. *Les Misérables* (Paris: Garnier Frères, 1963), Vol. II, p. 513.

8. *Ibid.*, p. 736.

9. Transl. Leonard Tancock (Harmondsworth: Penguin Books, 1954), p. 446.

10. See Citron, *La Poésie de Paris*, Vol. I, p. 250.

11. (Paris: Garnier Frères, 1963), p. 309.

12. In *The Works of Nathaniel Hawthorne* (Boston: Houghton Mifflin, Standard Library Edition, 1851), Vol. I, pp. 218-227.

13. "Der Dichter und diese Zeit," in *Ausgewählte Werke in zwei Bänden*, ed. Rudolf Hirsch (Frankfurt/Main: S. Fischer Verlag, 1957), Vol. II, p. 452.

14. *Oeuvres complètes* (Paris: NRF Gallimard, Bibliothèque de la Pléiade, 1961), p. 310.

15. In a fascinating article, Karlheinz Stierle has traced Baudelaire's "Tableaux parisiens" back to the moralising *tableau de Paris* as a subliterary genre of feuilletonistic literature which originated with Mercier's *Tableau de Paris*, which derived in turn from Diderot's dramatic theory. This article also sheds an interesting light on the concept of the urban *flâneur*. See Karlheinz Stierle, "Baudelaire and the Tradition of the *Tableau de Paris*," in *New Literary History*, XI, 2 (1980), 345-361. (Trans. of "Baudelaire's 'Tableaux parisiens' und die Tradition des 'tableau de Paris,' " *Poetica*, 6 [1974], 285-322.)

16. *Ibid.*, p. 78. This translation, like my others, aims for accuracy rather than beauty.

17. *Ibid.*, p. 1076.

18. *Ibid.*, p. 1083.

19. *Madame Bovary*, transl. Eleanor Marx Aveling, rev. Paul de Man (New York: W. W. Norton, Norton Critical Editions, 1965), p. 190 (Part Three, Ch. V).

20. "Il se muet dans l'immense sans vertige." "*Les Misérables* par Victor Hugo," in *Oeuvres complètes*, p. 786.

21. Citron notes that Paris had always, in literature, been regarded as a living being. After 1830 its gender changed, from predominantly feminine to predominantly masculine, so that at the moment when the myth of Paris

emerges full force, around 1830, "Paris becomes male in becoming dynamic." (*La Poésie de Paris*, Vol. II, pp. 7-9.)

22. *Les Misérables*, Vol. I, p. 158 (Part I, Book 3, Ch. 3).

23. *Notre Dame de Paris 1482*, ed. S. de Sacy (Paris: Gallimard, Collection Folio, 1966). "Ceci tuera cela," pp. 237-254 (Book V, Ch. 2).

24. *Ibid.*, p. 410 (Book VIII, Ch. 4).

25. On a less perceptive level, this same pattern is evident in *The Phantom of the Opera*.

26. *Notre Dame*, pp. 456-457 (Book IX, Ch. 7).

27. In *Oeuvres de Victor Hugo* (Paris: Alphonse Lemerre, 1875-1881), Vol. I, pp. 32-50.

28. François Rabelais, *The Histories of Gargantua and Pantagruel*, transl. J. M. Cohen (Baltimore: Penguin Books, 1955), p. 74 (Book I, Ch. 17).

29. This progression is too lengthy to be detailed here. One demonstration of it would be a comparison between the description of Tom-All-Alone's in *Bleak House* and that of Arthur Clennam's mother's house in *Little Dorrit*. The former is dramatized reporting, in which the dilapidated buildings are equated with the people who live in them. The latter plays an active role in the story, finally collapsing on the villain; it is the dramatic counterpart to the passive monument in *Little Dorrit*, the Marshalsea Prison. (The house is a prison too.)

30. *Our Mutual Friend*, ed. Stephen Gill (Harmondsworth: Penguin Books, 1971), p. 43 (Book I, Ch. 1).

31. *Ibid.*, pp. 104-105 (Book I, Ch. 6).

32. Anatole Broyard, review of *The English Pub* by Michael Jackson, in "Books of the Times," *New York Times*, August 30, 1976.

33. *Our Mutual Friend*, pp. 333-335 (Book II, Ch. 5). There is an interesting "topoanalysis" of the verticality of the house in psychological terms in Bachelard's *The Poetics of Space*, pp. 17-26.

34. *Our Mutual Friend*, pp. 267-268 (Book II, Ch. 1).

35. In *Sämtliche Werke*, ed. Ernst Zinn (Wiesbaden: Insel Verlag, 1955), Vol. I, pp. 721-722. "Vanity Fair" is of course a venerable topos in European literature. Another notable example, also connected with the city, occurs at the end of Book 7 of Wordsworth's *Prelude*.

Chapter III

1. For an interesting rumination on this subject, see Erich Heller, "The Artist's Journey into the Interior: A Hegelian Prophecy and its Fulfillment," in *The Artist's Journey into the Interior* (New York: Random House, Vintage Books, 1968), pp. 99-170.

2. *The American Scene*, p. 112.

3. *Oeuvres complètes*, pp. 81-83.

4. *À la recherche du temps perdu* (Paris: NRF Gallimard, Bibliothèque de la Pléiade, 1954), Vol. 3, p. 870.

5. For an account of the extent to which Paris was physically transformed between 1850 and 1870, see David H. Pinkney, *Napoleon III and the Rebuilding of Paris* (Princeton: Princeton University Press, 1958). The Paris Victor Hugo had known in his youth was still largely a medieval city.

6. 1856. I refer throughout to the 1881 version.

7. In *The Portable Walt Whitman*, ed. Mark van Doren, rev. Malcolm Cowley (New York: Viking Press, 1974), pp. 399-400.

8. See Edwin H. Miller, *Walt Whitman's Poetry, a Psychological Journey* (New York: New York University Press, 1968), pp. 200-207. There is an interesting discussion of "Crossing Brooklyn Ferry" in Quentin Anderson, *The Imperial Self* (New York: Random House, Vintage Books, 1971), pp. 119-165.

9. (New York: Random House, The Modern Library, 1956), p. 178.

10. *The Portable Walt Whitman*, pp. 326-328.

11. *The Complete Poems and Selected Letters and Prose of Hart Crane*, ed. Brom Weber (New York: Liveright, 1966), p. 89.

12. This author (1834-1882) should not be confused with his younger contemporary Francis Thompson, author of "The Hound of Heaven," or the earlier and more famous James Thomson (1700-1748), author of *The Seasons*. Edition cited: *The City of Dreadful Night and other Poems* (London: Bertram Dobell, 1910), pp. 1-50.

13. Don Martindale, "Prefatory Remarks," in Max Weber, *The City* (New York: The Free Press, 1958), p. 11.

14. Transl. Ralph E. Matlaw (New York: E. P. Dutton, 1960), p. 6.

15. "Dostoevsky in *Crime and Punishment*," *Partisan Review*, Vol. XXVII, No. 3, summer, 1960, pp. 393-425. Reprinted in Dostoevsky, *Crime and Punishment*, ed. George Gibian. Rev. ed. (New York: W. W. Norton, Norton Critical Editions, 1975), pp. 536-560.

16. N. P. Antsiferov, *Byl i mif Peterburga* (Petersburg, 1924), p. 57. Transl. and quoted in Donald Fanger, *Dostoevsky and Romantic Realism* (Chicago: University of Chicago Press, 1965), p. 295.

17. Transl. Jesse Coulson, ed. Gibian, pp. 429-430.

18. *Statyi za 1845-1868 gody*, in B. Tomashevsky and K. Khalabayev, eds., *Polnoye sobranie Rhudozhestvennykh sochinenii* (Moscow-Leningrad, 1930), Vol. XIII, p. 23. Transl. and quoted in Fanger, pp. 143-144.

19. "The Revolt against Mother Earth," in *Freedom and the Tragic Life* (New York: Noonday Press, 1952), pp. 72-85. Reprinted in *Crime and Punishment*, ed. Gibian, pp. 577-585; p. 578.

20. Ed. Gibian, Prefatory Note.

21. Dostoevsky, *The Notebooks for Crime and Punishment*, transl. and ed. Edward Wasiolek (Chicago: University of Chicago Press, 1967).

22. Ed. Gibian, p. 2.

23. Transl. John Cournos (New York: Grove Press, 1959), p. xxii. A new and more reliable translation of Biely's novel is *Petersburg*, transl. Robert A. Maguire and John E. Malmstad (Bloomington: Indiana Univ. Press, 1978).

24. *Ibid.*, p. 227.

25. *Ibid.*, p. 115.

26. *Ibid.*, p. 167.

Chapter IV

1. Rilke, *Die Aufzeichnungen des Malte Laurids Brigge*, in *Sämtliche Werke*, ed. Ernst Zinn (Frankfurt/Main: Insel, 1966), Vol. VI, p. 709; my translation. Mrs. Norton's translation seems to me to miss the harsh, rough abruptness with which Malte records his perception of the city. Rilke presents this aspect toughly, in a hard style; Mrs. Norton nudges the reader in a more belletristic direction.

2. In T. S. Eliot, *Collected Poems, 1909-1935* (New York: Harcourt Brace, 1936), p. 14.

3. See Hugh Kenner, "The Urban Apocalypse," in *Eliot in his Time*, ed. A. Walton Litz (Princeton: Princeton University Press, 1973), pp. 23-49.

4. *Ibid.*, p. 46.

5. Chapter IV in Henri Lefebvre, *Everyday Life in the Modern World*, transl. Sacha Rabinovitch (New York: Harper and Row, Harper Torchbooks, 1971).

6. Transl. Willa and Edwin Muir, rev. E. M. Butler (New York: Schocken Books, 1968), p. 34.

7. For a discussion of the larger theme of Italy in German literature, of which the Venice topos is part, see Paul Requadt, *Die Bildersprache der deutschen Italiendichtung von Goethe bis Benn* (Bern: Francke, 1962).

8. See my article, "Thomas Mann and the Problematic Self," in *Publications of the English Goethe Society*, Vol. XXXVII, 1967, pp. 120-141.

9. Transl. H. T. Lowe-Porter (New York: Random House, Vintage Books, 1964), p. 12.

10. In Nietzsche's city poem "Venedig," the speaker is isolated from a community. In his philosophical works Nietzsche is unremittingly hostile to the big city, although Venice occupies a special corner of his affection. His most extensive philippic against the city in general occurs in *Also sprach Zarathustra*, Part III, "Vom Vorübergehen" ("Of Passing By"), in *Werke in drei Bänden*, ed. Karl Schlechta (München: Carl Hanser, 1966), Vol. II, pp. 425-428.

11. *Sociology as an Art Form*, p. 45. For an interesting discussion of the

background of Freud's *Group Psychology* (*Massenpsychologie*), see Philip Rieff, *Freud: The Mind of the Moralist*, 3rd ed. (Chicago: Univ. of Chicago Press, 1979), pp. 228-233.

12. *Culture and Society* (London: Chatto and Windus, 1958), p. 300. Quoted in Meyersohn, p. 9.

13. Rolf Meyersohn, "Social Ignorance and Social Order in City Life," unpublished paper delivered at the Colloquium concerning the Continuity of Cities, American Embassy, London, October 28, 1967, p. 9. I am grateful to Professor Meyersohn for giving me a copy of his paper.

14. The quotation and points in this sentence from Meyersohn, p. 10.

15. Henry James notes that "it was the fortune, it was in a manner the doom, of Les Rougon-Macquart to deal with things almost always in gregarious form, to be a picture of *numbers*, of classes, crowds, confusions, movements, industries." "Émile Zola," in *Notes on Novelists* (New York: Biblo and Tannen, 1969), p. 35.

16. "Der Gott der Stadt," in *Dichtungen und Schriften, Gesamtausgabe in vier Bänden*, ed. Karl Ludwig Schneider (Hamburg: Ellermann, 1960ff.), Vol. I (1964), p. 192. This poem defies adequate translation because of Heym's typically Expressionist attempt to deconstruct the standard syntactic patterns of German.

17. *St. Petersburg*, pp. 198-199.

18. In *Gesammelte Werke in neun Bänden*, ed. Frisé, Vol. II, pp. 628-629 (Book I, Part I, Chapter 120). For a more detailed presentation of this scene and its context, see my article, "Musil and the City," in *Musil-Forum*, 5. Jhrg. 1979, 1. Halbjahrsheft, pp. 68-87.

19. *Ibid.*, p. 647 (Chapter 122).

20. *Ibid.*

Chapter V

1. *The Secular City*, p. 16.

2. See M. H. Abrams, *Natural Supernaturalism: Tradition and Revolution in Romantic Literature* (New York: W. W. Norton, 1971).

3. For a penetrating discussion of art's appropriation of entropy, see Rudolf Arnheim, *Entropy and Art: An Essay on Order and Disorder* (Berkeley: Univ. of California Press, 1971). On the withering away of determinism in physics, see Richard Schlegel, "Physics, The most Important of the Liberal Arts," *The Key Reporter* (Phi Beta Kappa) XLV, 3, spring 1980, pp. 2-4. On randomness and society, see Alfred M. Bork, "Randomness and the Twentieth Century," *Antioch Review*, 27, 1967, pp. 40-61.

4. *The Image of the City*, p. 126.

5. I am prepared to argue that *The Castle* is really a city novel, in spite of

the fact that its community is unequivocally called a "Dorf" (village). The spatial dimensions of this place are too large, the lines of communication too tenuous, the castle too remote for a village. I think what Kafka has done is to skeletonize a city, reducing it to its schematic elements (monument/authority/everyday life/closed society/outsider) in order to abstract the attempt of K., the stranger from outside, to penetrate its magic center, the castle itself.

6. As cited by Joseph Frank in his essay, "Spatial Form in Modern Literature," in *The Widening Gyre* (New Brunswick: Rutgers University Press, 1963), pp. 3-62. For a brief summary of the current critical interest in spatiality, see Jeffrey R. Smitten, "Approaches to the Spatiality of Narrative," in *PLL: Papers on Language and Literature*, 14, 3, summer 1978, pp. 296-314. (Smitten overlooks the seminal influence of Walter Benjamin.) See also Joseph A. Kestner, *The Spatiality of the Novel* (Detroit: Wayne State University Press, 1978) and a penetrating short essay by Gérard Genette, "La littérature et l'espace," in *Figures II* (Paris: Éditions du Seuil, 1969), pp. 43-48.

7. In *Bertolt Brecht: Poems, 1913-1956*, ed. John Willett and Ralph Manheim, with the cooperation of Erich Fried (New York: Methuen, 1979), pp. 107-108. This translation is used for reasons of copyright, although a more literal one would be more appropriate for my argument.

8. Thus *"die langen Gehäuse,"* "long housings," and *"Eiland,"* "isle"; the former is more nuanced than Willett's "boxes," and the latter more accurate. On the myth of Manhattan in German literature, see e.g. Sigrid Bauschinger, "Mythos Manhattan. Die Faszination einer Stadt," in *Amerika in der deutschen Literatur: Neue Welt—Nordamerika—USA* (Stuttgart: Reclam, 1975).

9. Bachelard, *The Poetics of Space*, p. 6.

10. *The Decline of the West*, transl. Charles Francis Atkinson (New York: Alfred A. Knopf, 1966). Spengler's central sermon on the city is in Vol. II, pp. 85-186.

11. Transl. Lloyd Alexander (New York: New Directions, 1964), p. 156.

12. Transl. William Weaver (New York: Harcourt Brace Jovanovich, 1974), p. 44.

13. Anselm L. Strauss, "Strategies for Discovering Urban Theory," in Anselm L. Strauss, ed., *The American City: A Sourcebook of Urban Imagery* (Chicago: Aldine Publishing Co., 1968), p. 518.

14. *Invisible Cities*, p. 138.

15. *Ibid.*, pp. 138-139.

16. See Kevin Lynch, *The Image of the City*.

17. *The American Scene*, pp. 139-140.

18. See Wohl and Strauss, "Symbolic Representation and the Urban Milieu," and Lynch, *The Image of the City*.

151

19. *The Home of Man* (New York: W. W. Norton, 1976), p. 29.

20. The term is Eliel Saarinen's, in *The City, its Growth, its Decay, its Future* (Cambridge, Mass.: The M.I.T. Press, 1943), p. 151.

21. (New York: Harcourt Brace Jovanovich, 1970), pp. 150-152.

22. Strauss, "Strategies for Discovering Urban Theory," p. 520.

23. Spengler, *The Decline of the West*, Vol. II, p. 102.

24. "Strategies for Discovering Urban Theory," p. 520.

25. *Sociology as an Art Form*, ch. 5.

26. H. W. Eldredge, as quoted in *The New York Times*, Jan. 8, 1979.

27. *The Culture of Cities*, p. 217.

28. "A Reporter at Large: The Towers of Light," in *The New Yorker*, July 10, 1978, pp. 32-58.

29. *Ibid.*, p. 44.

30. *Ibid.*, p. 58.

31. *Ibid.*, p. 52. Actually, the phenomenon is not so recent; it goes back at least to Richard Jeffries' *After London* (1885).

32. *Ibid.*, pp. 54-55.

33. *Ibid.*, p. 55.

34. Transl. Gregory Rabassa (New York: Harper and Row, 1970), p. 422.

35. "Das wahre Bild der Vergangenheit *huscht* vorbei. Nur als Bild, das auf Nimmerwiedersehen im Augenblick seiner Erkennbarkeit eben aufblitzt, ist die Vergangenheit festzuhalten." "Über den Begriff der Geschichte," in *Gesammelte Werke*, ed. Rolf Tiedemann and Hermann Schweppenhäuser (Frankfurt/Main: Suhrkamp, 1974), Bd. I, Teil 2, p. 695.

Conclusion

1. *La Torre di Babele*, 3rd ed. (Padova: Marsilio Editori, 1974), pp. 178-179.

2. *Invisible Cities*, p. 127.

3. In *City Life* (New York: Farrar, Straus and Giroux, 1970), pp. 166-167.

4. (New York: Alfred A. Knopf, 1979), p. 67.

BIBLIOGRAPHY

Abrams, M. H. *Natural Supernaturalism: Tradition and Revolution in Romantic Literature*. New York: W. W. Norton, 1971.

———, et al., eds. *The Norton Anthology of English Literature*. 2 vols. New York: W. W. Norton, 1962.

Ahearn, Edward J. "The Search for Community: The City in Hölderlin, Wordsworth, and Baudelaire." *Texas Studies in Literature and Language*, 13, No. 1 (1971), 71-89.

Anderson, Quentin. *The Imperial Self*. New York: Random House, Vintage Books, 1971.

Antsiferov, N. P. *Byl i mif Peterburga*. Petersburg, 1924.

Arnheim, Rudolf. *Entropy and Art: An Essay on Order and Disorder*. Berkeley: Univ. of California Press, 1971.

Auden, W. H. "The Poet and the City" in *The Dyer's Hand*. New York: Random House, Vintage Books, 1968.

Bachelard, Gaston. *The Poetics of Space*, transl. Maria Jolas. Boston: Beacon Press, 1969.

Balzac, Honoré de. *Illusions perdues*, ed. A. Adam. Paris: Garnier Frères, 1961.

———. *Le Père Goriot*. Paris: Garnier Frères, 1963.

Barthelme, Donald. *City Life*. New York: Farrar, Straus and Giroux, 1970.

Baudelaire, Charles. *Les Fleurs du mal*, in *Oeuvres complètes*. Paris: NRF Gallimard, Bibliothèque de la Pléiade, 1961.

———. "*Les Misérables* par Victor Hugo." *Ibid*.

———. *Le Peintre de la vie moderne*. *Ibid*.

———. *Salon de 1859*. *Ibid*.

———. *Le Spleen de Paris*. *Ibid*.

Bauschinger, Sigrid. "Mythos Manhattan. Die Faszination einer Stadt," in *Amerika in der deutschen Literatur: Neue Welt—Nordamerika—USA*, ed. S. Bauschinger, H. Denkler, W. Malsch. Stuttgart: Philipp Reclam jun., 1975.

Becker, Carl L. *The Heavenly City of the Eighteenth-Century Philosophers.* New Haven: Yale Univ. Press, 1932.

Benjamin, Walter. *Charles Baudelaire: Ein Lyriker im Zeitalter des Hochkapitalismus*, ed. Rolf Tiedemann. Frankfurt/Main: Suhrkamp Verlag, 1974.

―――. "Paris—Capital of the Nineteenth Century," in *New Left Review*, No. 48 (Mar.-Apr. 1968), 72-88.

―――. "Über den Begriff der Geschichte," in *Gesammelte Werke*, ed. Rolf Tiedemann and Hermann Schweppenhäuser, Vol. I, Part 2. Frankfurt/Main: Suhrkamp Verlag, 1974.

Biely, Andrey. *St. Petersburg*, transl. John Cournos. New York: Grove Press, 1959.

Blume, Bernhard. "Die Stadt als seelische Landschaft im Werk Rainer Maria Rilkes," in *Monatshefte für deutsche Unterricht*, Vol. 43 (1951), 65-82, 133-149.

Bork, Alfred M. "Randomness and the Twentieth Century." *Antioch Review*, 27 (1967), 40-61.

Braudel, Fernand. *Capitalism and Material Life, 1400-1800*, transl. Miriam Kochan. New York: Harper and Row, 1973.

Brecht, Bertolt. "Vom armen B. B.," in *Bertolt Brechts Hauspostille.* Berlin: Suhrkamp Verlag, 1960.

Brooks, Peter. *The Melodramatic Imagination: Balzac, Henry James, Melodrama, and the Mode of Excess.* New Haven: Yale Univ. Press, 1976.

Broyard, Anatole. Rev. of *The English Pub* by Michael Jackson. *New York Times.* Aug. 30, 1976.

Burke, Kenneth. *Counterstatement.* Berkeley: Univ. of California Press, 1968.

Butor, Michel. *Répertoire III.* Paris: Éditions de Minuit, 1968.

Byrd, Max. *London Transformed: Images of the City in the Eighteenth Century.* New Haven: Yale Univ. Press, 1978.

Caillois, Roger. "Balzac et le mythe de Paris," in *l'Ouevre de Balzac*, ed. A. Béguin. Paris, 1950, Vol. 4, i-xvii.

―――. *Le mythe et l'homme.* Nouvelle édition. Paris: Gallimard, 1972.

Calvino, Italo. *Invisible Cities*, transl. William Weaver. New York: Harcourt Brace Jovanovich, 1972.

Citron, Pierre. *La Poésie de Paris dans la littérature française de Rousseau à Baudelaire*. 2 vols. Paris: Éditions de Minuit, 1961.

Coulanges, Fustel de. *La Cité antique*. Paris: Hachette, 1880.

Cox, Harvey. *The Secular City: Secularization and Urbanization in Theological Perspective*. Rev. ed. New York: Macmillan, 1968.

Crane, Hart. *The Complete Poems and Selected Letters and Prose of Hart Crane*, ed. Brom Weber. New York: Liveright, 1966.

Curtius, Ernst Robert. *European Literature and the Latin Middle Ages*, transl. Willard R. Trask. New York: Harper and Row, 1953.

Day, Robert A. "The 'City Man' in *The Waste Land*: The Geography of Reminiscence," in *PLMA*, 80 (1965), 285-291.

de Man, Paul. "The Rhetoric of Temporality," in *Interpretation: Theory and Practice*, ed. Charles Singleton. Baltimore: Johns Hopkins Univ. Press, 1969.

De Quincey, Thomas. "The Nation of London," in *Autobiographical Sketches*. Boston: Houghton Mifflin, 1854.

Dickens, Charles. *Our Mutual Friend*, ed. Stephen Gill. Harmondsworth: Penguin Books, 1971.

Dostoevsky, Fyodor. *Crime and Punishment*, transl. Jesse Coulson, ed. George Gibian. Rev. ed. New York: W. W. Norton, 1975.

———. *The Notebooks for Crime and Punishment*, transl. and ed. Edward Wasiolek. Chicago: Univ. of Chicago Press, 1967.

———. *Notes from Underground*, transl. Ralph E. Matlaw. New York: E. P. Dutton, 1960.

———. *Statyi za 1845-1868 gody*, in *Polnoye sobranie Rhudozhestvennykh sochinenii*, ed. B. Tomashevsky and K. Khalabayev. Moscow-Leningrad, 1930, Vol. XIII, p. 23.

Dougherty, James. *The Fivesquare City: The City in the Religious Imagination*. Notre Dame: Univ. of Notre Dame Press, 1980.

Dryden, John. *The Poems of John Dryden*, ed. John Sargeant. London: Geoffrey Cumberledge/Oxford Univ. Press, 1910.

Eliade, Mircea. *Cosmos and History: The Myth of the Eternal Return*, transl. Willard R. Trask. New York: Harper and Row, 1959.

Eliot, T. S. *Collected Poems, 1909-1935*. New York: Harcourt Brace, 1936.

Ellul, Jacques. *The Meaning of the City*, transl. Dennis Pardee. Grand Rapids: William B. Eerdmans, 1970.

Fanger, Donald. *Dostoevsky and Romantic Realism: A Study of Dostoevsky in Relation to Balzac, Dickens, and Gogol*. Chicago: Univ. of Chicago Press, 1967.

Festa-McCormick, Diana. *The City as Catalyst*. Rutherford: Fairleigh Dickinson Univ. Press, 1979.

Flaubert, Gustave. *l'Éducation sentimentale*, ed. Éd. Maynial. Paris: Garnier Frères, 1964.

————. *Madame Bovary*, transl. Eleanor Marx Aveling, rev. Paul de Man. New York: W. W. Norton, 1965.

Frank, Joseph. "Spatial Form in Modern Literature," in *The Widening Gyre*. New Brunswick: Rutgers Univ. Press, 1963.

Freud, Sigmund. *Civilization and Its Discontents*, transl. and ed. James Strachey. New York: W. W. Norton, 1962.

————. *The Interpretation of Dreams*, transl. and ed. James Strachey. New York: Avon Books, 1965.

————. *Totem and Taboo*, transl. James Strachey. New York: W. W. Norton, 1950.

Fries, Marilyn Bibley. "Literary Reflections: The Image of Berlin in the German Novel from Raabe to Döblin." Diss. Cornell, 1975.

Fritz, Paul, comp. *City and Society in the Eighteenth Century*, ed. Paul Fritz and David Williams. Proceedings of the McMaster Univ. Association for Eighteenth Century Studies, Vol. 3. Toronto: Hakkert, 1973.

Frye, Northrop. *The Anatomy of Criticism*. Princeton: Princeton Univ. Press, 1957.

Garber, Frederick. "Time and the City in Rilke's *Malte Laurids Brigge*." *Contemporary Literature*, Vol. 11, 3 (1970), 324-339.

Gardet, L., *et al. Cultures and Time*. Paris: The UNESCO Press, 1976.

Gelfant, Blanche. *The American City Novel*, 2nd ed. Norman: Univ. of Oklahoma Press, 1970.

————. "Residence Underground: Recent Fictions of the Subterranean City." *Sewanee Review*, 83 (1975), 406-438.

Gelley, Alexander. "Metonymy, Schematism, and the Space of Literature." *New Literary History* XI (1979-80), 469-487.

Gibson, J. J. *The Ecological Approach to Visual Perception*. Boston: Houghton Mifflin, 1979.

Gombrich, E. H. *Art and Illusion: A Study in the Psychology of Pictorial Representation*, 2nd ed. Princeton: Princeton Univ. Press, Bollingen Series XXXV, 5, 1961.

Gordon, Felicia Morris. "The Wonderful Immensity: A Comparative Study of the City in Dickens and Balzac." Diss. Berkeley, 1974.

Halbwachs, Maurice. *La Topographie légendaire des Évangiles en Terre Sainte, étude de mémoire collective.* Paris: Presses universitaires de France, 1941.

Hamm, Michael F., ed. *The City in Russian History.* Lexington: Univ. of Kentucky Press, 1976.

Hammond, Mason. *The City in the Ancient World.* Cambridge, Mass.: Harvard Univ. Press, 1972.

Handlin, Oscar, and John Burchard, eds. *The Historian and the City.* Cambridge, Mass.: M.I.T. Press, 1963.

Hartman, Geoffrey H. *Wordsworth's Poetry, 1787-1814.* New Haven: Yale Univ. Press, 1977.

Hawthorne, Nathaniel. "The Grey Champion," in *The Works of Nathaniel Hawthorne,* Standard Library Edition. Boston: Houghton Mifflin, 1851, Vol. 1.

———. "Sights from a Steeple," in *The Complete Works of Nathaniel Hawthorne,* Riverside Edition. Boston: Houghton Mifflin, 1882-98, Vol. I.

Hay, Dennis. *The Medieval Centuries.* New York: Harper and Row, 1964.

Heller, Erich. *The Artist's Journey into the Interior.* New York: Random House, 1968.

Heym, Georg. *Dichtungen und Schriften: Gesamtausgabe in vier Bänden,* ed. Karl Ludwig Schneider. Hamburg: Heinrich Ellermann Verlag, 1960ff.

Hofmannsthal, Hugo von. *Aufzeichnungen,* in *Gesammelte Werke in Einzelausgaben,* ed. Herbert Steiner. Frankfurt/Main: S. Fischer Verlag, 1959.

———. *Ausgewählte Werke in zwei Bänden,* ed. Rudolph Hirsch. Frankfurt/Main: S. Fischer Verlag, 1957.

Howe, Irving. "The City in Literature." *Commentary,* 51, No. 5 (1971), 61-68.

Hugo, Victor. "À l'Arc de Triomphe," in *Oeuvres de Victor Hugo.* Paris: Alphonse Lemerre, 1875-1881, Vol. 1.

Hugo, Victor. *Notre Dame de Paris 1482*, ed. S. de Sacy. Paris: Gallimard, 1966.

——. *Les Misérables*, ed. M.-F. Guyard. 2 vols. Paris: Garnier Frères, 1963.

Ivanov, Vyacheslav. "The Revolt against Mother Earth," in *Freedom and the Tragic Life*. New York: Noonday Press, 1952. Rpt. in Dostoevsky, *Crime and Punishment*, ed. Gibian.

James, Henry. *The Ambassadors*. Harmondsworth: Penguin Books, 1973.

——. *The American Scene*. Bloomington: Indiana Univ. Press, 1969.

——. *The Bostonians*. New York: Random House, 1956.

Jones, Ernest. *The Life and Works of Sigmund Freud*. 3 vols. New York: Basic Books, 1955.

Kafka, Franz. *The Trial*, transl. Willa and Edwin Muir, rev. E. M. Butler. New York: Schocken Books, 1968.

Kenner, Hugh. "The Urban Apocalypse," in *Eliot in his Time*, ed. A. Walton Litz. Princeton: Princeton Univ. Press, 1973, 23-49.

Kestner, Joseph A. *The Spatiality of the Novel*. Detroit: Wayne State Univ. Press, 1978.

Klotz, Volker. *Die erzählte Stadt: Ein Sujet als Herausforderung des Romans von Lesage bis Döblin*. Munich: Carl Hanser Verlag, 1969.

Konrád, George. *The City Builder*, transl. Ivan Sanders. New York: Harcourt Brace Jovanovich, 1978.

Koolhaas, Rem. *Delirious New York*. New York: Oxford Univ. Press, 1978.

Lefebvre, Henri. *Everyday Life in the Modern World*, transl. Sacha Rabinovitch. New York: Harper and Row, 1971.

Legget, Robert F. *Cities and Geology*. New York: McGraw-Hill, 1973.

Lessard, Suzannah. "The Towers of Light." *The New Yorker*, July 10, 1978, 32-58.

Lucas, J. R. *A Treatise on Time and Space*. London: Methuen, 1973.

Lurie, Alison. *The Nowhere City*. New York: Coward-McCann, 1966.

Lynch, Kevin. *The Image of the City*. Cambridge, Mass.: M.I.T. Press, 1960.

Mann, Thomas. *Death in Venice*, transl. H. T. Lowe-Porter. New York: Random House, 1964.

Márquez, Gabriel García. *One Hundred Years of Solitude*, transl. Gregory Rabassa. New York: Harper and Row, 1970.

Marx, Leo. *The Machine in the Garden: Technology and the Pastoral Ideal in America*. New York: Oxford Univ. Press, 1964.

Mayhew, Henry. *London Labour and the London Poor*. New York: A. M. Kelley, 1967.

Mellaart, James. "The Origins and Development of Cities in the Near East," in *Janus: Essays in Ancient and Modern Studies*, ed. Louis L. Orlin. Ann Arbor: Center for Coordination of Ancient and Modern Studies, Univ. of Michigan, 1975, 5-22.

Mercer, Charles. *Living in Cities: Psychology and the Urban Environment*. Harmondsworth: Penguin Books, 1975.

Meyersohn, Rolf. "Social Ignorance and Social Order in City Life." Colloquium concerning the Continuity of Cities, American Embassy, London, Oct. 28, 1967.

Miller, Edwin H. *Walt Whitman's Poetry, A Psychological Journey*. New York: New York Univ. Press, 1968.

Minder, Robert. "Paris in der französischen Literatur (1760-1960)," in *Dichter in der Gesellschaft*. Frankfurt/Main: Insel Verlag, 1966, 287-340.

Mitchell, W.T.J. "Spatial Form in Modern Literature: Toward a General Theory." *Critical Inquiry* 6 (spring 1980), 539-567.

Moorman, Mary. *William Wordsworth, A Biography*. 2 vols. Oxford: Clarendon Press, 1957-65.

Mumford, Lewis. *The City in History: Its Origins, its Transformations, and its Prospects*. New York: Harcourt Brace and World, 1961.

———. *The Culture of Cities*. New York: Harcourt Brace Jovanovich, 1970.

Murray, Henry A., ed, *Myth and Mythmaking*, Boston: Beacon Press, 1968.

Musil, Robert. *Der Mann ohne Eigenschaften*, in *Gesammelte Werke in neun Bänden*, ed. Adolf Frisé. Reinbek bei Hamburg: Rowohlt Verlag, 1978, vols. 1-5.

Naipaul, V. S. *A Bend in the River*. New York: Alfred A. Knopf, 1979.

Nerlich, Graham. *The Shape of Space*. Cambridge: Cambridge Univ. Press, 1976.

Nietzsche, Friedrich. *Werke in drei Bänden*, ed. Karl Schlechta. Munich: Carl Hanser Verlag, 1966.

Nisbet, Robert. *Sociology as an Art Form*. New York: Oxford Univ. Press, 1976.

O'Bryon, Patrick. "Response to the Urban Challenge: The Search for Home in the City in the Twentieth-Century German Novel." Diss. Princeton, 1976.

Oswald, Hans. *Die überschätzte Stadt: Ein Beitrag der Gemeindesoziologie zum Städtebau*, ed. Heinrich Popitz. Olten: Walter Verlag, 1966.

Park, Robert E., Ernest W. Burgess, and Robert D. McKenzie. *The City*. Chicago: Univ. of Chicago Press, 1967.

Pike, Burton. "Thomas Mann and the Problematic Self." *Publications of the English Goethe Society* 37 (1967), 120-141.

Pinkney, David H. *Napoleon III and the Rebuilding of Paris*. Princeton: Princeton Univ. Press, 1972.

Proust, Marcel. *À la recherche du temps perdu*. 3 vols. Paris: NRF Gallimard, Bibliothèque de la Pléiade, 1954.

Pushkin, Alexander. *Le Cavalier de Bronze: Nouvelle pétersbourgeoise, 1833*, transl. and ed. André Meynieux. N.p.: Editions André Bonne, Cahiers d'Études littéraires, 1959.

Quaroni, Ludovico. *La Torre di Babele*. 3rd ed. Padua: Marsilio Editore, 1974.

Rabelais, François. *The Histories of Gargantua and Pantagruel*, transl. J. M. Cohen. Baltimore: Penguin Books, 1955.

Rahv, Philip. "Dostoevsky in *Crime and Punishment*." *Partisan Review* 27, No. 3 (1960), 393-425. Rpt. in Dostoevsky, *Crime and Punishment*, ed. Gibian.

Requadt, Paul. *Die Bildersprache der deutschen Italiendichtung von Goethe bis Benn*. Bern: Francke Verlag, 1962.

Richardson, Joanna. *The Bohemians: La Vie de Bohème in Paris, 1830-1914*. South Brunswick: A. S. Barnes, 1971.

Righter, William. *Myth and Literature*. London and Boston: Routledge and Kegan Paul, 1975.

Rilke, Rainer Maria. *Die Aufzeichnungen des Malte Laurids Brigge*, in *Sämtliche Werke*, ed. Ernst Zinn, Vol. 6. Frankfurt/Main: Insel Verlag, 1966.

———. *Duineser Elegien*. *Ibid*. Vol. 1, 1955.

Rykwert, Joseph. *The Idea of a Town: The Anthropology of Urban Form in Rome, Italy, and the Ancient World*. Princeton: Princeton Univ. Press, 1976.

Saarinen, Eliel. *The City, its Growth, its Decay, its Future*. Cambridge, Mass.: M.I.T. Press, 1943.

Sachs, Curt. *Rhythm and Tempo: A Study in Music History*. New York: W. W. Norton, 1953.

Sansot, Pierre. *Poétique de la Ville*. Paris: Éditions Klincksieck, 1971.

Schilling, Bernard N. *The Hero as Failure: Balzac and the Rubempré Cycle*. Chicago: Univ. of Chicago Press, 1968.

Schlegel, Richard. "Physics, The most Important of the Liberal Arts." *The Key Reporter* (Phi Beta Kappa) XLV, 3 (1980), 2-4.

Schorske, Carl E. "The Idea of the City in European Thought: Voltaire to Spengler," in *The Historian and the City*, ed. Oscar Handlin and John Burchard. Cambridge, Mass.: M.I.T. Press, 1963, 94-114.

Schwarzbach, Fredric. *Dickens and the City*. London: Athlone Press, 1978.

Sennett, Richard. *The Fall of Public Man: On the Social Psychology of Capitalism*. New York: Random House, 1978.

Sica, Paolo. *L'immagine della città da Sparta a Las Vegas*. Bari: Editori Laterza, 1970.

Sjoberg, Gideon. "The Preindustrial City." *American Journal of Sociology*, 60, No. 4 (1955), 438-445.

Simmel, Georg. "The Metropolis and Mental Life," in *The Sociology of Georg Simmel*, ed. Kurt Wolff. Glencoe: Free Press, 1950, 409-424.

Smitten, Jeffrey R. "Approaches to the Spatiality of Narrative." *PLL: Papers on Language and Literature*, 14, No. 3 (1978), 296-314.

Spears, Monroe K. *Dionysus and the City: Modernism in Twentieth-Century Poetry*. New York: Oxford Univ. Press, 1970.

Spengler, Osward. *The Decline of the West*, transl. Charles Francis Atkinson. 2 vols. New York: Alfred A. Knopf, 1966.

States, Bert O. "The Persistence of the Archetype." *Critical Inquiry* 7 (winter 1980), 333-344.

Stewart, Terence Charles. *The City as an Image of Man*. London: Latimer Press, 1970.

Stout, Janis P. *Sodoms in Eden: The City in American Fiction before 1860*. Contributions in American Studies 19. Westport, Conn.: Greenwood Press, 1976.

Strauss, Anselm L. "Strategies for Discovering Urban Theory," in *The American City: A Sourcebook of Urban Imagery*, ed. Anselm L. Strauss. Chicago: Aldine Publishing Co., 1968, 515-530.

161

Sue, Eugène. *Les Mystères de Paris. Présentation par Jean-Louis Bory* [Édition intégrale]. Paris: Jean-Jacques Pauvert, 1963.

Thalmann, Marianne. *Romantiker entdecken die Stadt.* Munich: Nymphenburger Verlag, 1965.

Thomson, James. *The City of Dreadful Night and other Poems.* London: Bertram Dobell, 1910.

Trautmann, Rene. *Die Stadt in der deutschen Erzählungskunst des neunzehnten Jahrhunderts (1830-1880).* Winterthur: Keller Verlag, 1957.

Vickery, John B., ed. *Myth and Literature: Contemporary Theory and Practice.* Lincoln: Univ. of Nebraska Press, 1966.

Voltaire. *Romans et contes,* ed. Henri Bénac. Paris: Garnier Frères, 1949.

Ward, Barbara. *The Home of Man.* New York: W. W. Norton, 1976.

Watt, Ian. *The Rise of the Novel.* Berkeley: Univ. of California Press, 1957.

Weber, Max. *The City,* transl. and ed. Don Martindale and Gertrud Neuwirth. New York: Free Press, 1958.

Weimer, David R. *The City as Metaphor.* New York: Random House, 1966.

Weiss, John. *The Origins of Modern Consciousness.* Detroit: Wayne State Univ. Press, 1965.

Welsh, Alexander. *The City of Dickens.* Oxford: Clarendon Press, 1971.

White, Morton, and Lucia White. *The Intellectual versus the City: From Thomas Jefferson to Frank Lloyd Wright.* New York: New American Library, 1962.

Whitman, Cedric. *Homer and the Homeric Tradition.* New York: W. W. Norton, 1958.

Whitman, Walt. "Crossing Brooklyn Ferry," in *Leaves of Grass and Selected Prose,* ed. Sculley Bradley. New York: Rinehart, 1958.

———. *The Portable Walt Whitman,* ed. Mark van Doren, rev. Malcolm Cowley. New York: Viking Press, 1974.

Williams, Raymond. *The Country and the City.* New York: Oxford Univ. Press, 1973.

———. *Culture and Society.* London: Chatto and Windus, 1958.

Wohl, R. Richard, and Anselm L. Strauss. "Symbolic Representation and the Urban Milieu." *American Journal of Sociology,* 63, No. 5 (1958), 523-532.

Zola, Émile. *Germinal,* transl. Leonard Tancock. Harmondsworth: Penguin Books, 1954.

INDEX

165

The Orbit of Thomas Mann. By Erich Kahler

On Four Modern Humanists: Hofmannsthal, Gundolf, Curtius, Kantorowicz. Edited by Arthur R. Evans, Jr.

Flaubert and Joyce: The Rite of Fiction. By Richard Cross

A Stage for Poets: Studies in the Theatre of Hugo and Musset. By Charles Affron

Hofmannsthal's Novel "Andreas." By David H. Miles

Kazantzakis and the Linguistic Revolution in Greek Literature. By Peter Bien

Modern Greek Writers. Edited by Edmund Keeley and Peter Bien

On Gide's Prométhée: Private Myth and Public Mystification. By Kurt Weinberg

The Inner Theatre of Recent French Poetry. By Mary Ann Caws

Wallace Stevens and the Symbolist Imagination. By Michel Benamou

Cervantes' Christian Romance: A Study of "Persiles y Sigismunda." By Alban K. Forcione

The Prison-House of Language: A Critical Account of Structuralism and Formalism. By Fredric Jameson

Ezra Pound and the Troubadour Tradition. By Stuart Y. McDougal

Wallace Stevens: Imagination and Faith. By Adalaide K. Morris

On the Art of Medieval Arabic Literature. By Andras Hamori

The Poetic World of Boris Pasternak. By Olga Hughes

The Aesthetics of György Lukács. By Béla Királyfalvi

The Echoing Wood of Theodore Roethke. By Jenijoy La Belle

Achilles' Choice: Examples of Modern Tragedy. By David Lenson

The Figure of Faust in Valéry and Goethe. By Kurt Weinberg

The Situation of Poetry: Contemporary Poetry and Its Traditions. By Robert Pinsky

The Symbolic Imagination: Coleridge and the Romantic Tradition. By J. Robert Barth, S.J.

Adventures in the Deeps of the Mind: The Cuchulain Cycle of W. B. Yeats. By Barton R. Friedman

Shakespearean Representation: Mimesis and Modernity of Elizabethan Tragedy. By Howard Felperin

René Char: The Myth and the Poem. By James R. Lawler

The German Bildungsroman from Wieland to Hesse. By Martin Swales

Six French Poets of Our Time: A Critical and Historical Study. By Robert W. Greene

Coleridge's Metaphors of Being. By Edward Kessler

The Lost Center and Other Essays in Greek Poetry. By Zissimos Lorenzatos

Shakespeare's Revisions of "King Lear". By Steven Urkowitz

Coleridge and the Language of Poetry. By Emerson Marks

Library of Congress Cataloging in Publication Data

Pike, Burton.
The image of the city in modern literature.

(Princeton essays in literature)
Bibliography: p. 153
Includes index.
1. Cities and towns in literature. 2. Literature, Modern—19th century—History and criticism. 3. Literature, Modern—20th century—History and criticism. I. Title. II. Series.
PN56.C55P54   809′.93321732   81-47149
ISBN 0-691-06488-1   AACR2

168